When We Were Pioneers

R Ruesch
Psalm 45:1

Robert N. Ruesch

ISBN 978-1-64492-269-9 (paperback)
ISBN 978-1-64492-270-5 (digital)

Copyright © 2019 by Robert N. Ruesch

All rights reserved. No part of this publication may be reproduced, distributed, or transmitted in any form or by any means, including photocopying, recording, or other electronic or mechanical methods without the prior written permission of the publisher. For permission requests, solicit the publisher via the address below.

Christian Faith Publishing, Inc.
832 Park Avenue
Meadville, PA 16335
www.christianfaithpublishing.com

Photographs are the property of The YMCA of the Rockies, Lula W. Dorsey Museum unless otherwise noted.

Printed in the United States of America

Robert N. Ruesch brings a very special perspective to an extraordinary place—Snow Mountain Ranch, YMCA of the Rockies. Bob was part of the leadership team that created the warm, enriching atmosphere of this YMCA center for families and conferences high in the Rocky Mountains. Additionally, Bob shares his personal growth in his years at Snow Mountain Ranch, helping to form the faithful servant he is today. I recommend his book for all who enjoy Snow Mountain Ranch today.
—M. Kent Meyer, Managing Director of
Snow Mountain Ranch, 1987–2001

Wonderful. It brought back so many great memories during simpler times. From the very beginning, the purchase of Snow Mountain Ranch and the legacy left by Rudy and Clarabelle Just. Dick Engle, the first managing director, along with his wife, Sylvia, and their two daughters, Cindy and Patrice, sharing their love of SMR.

Endearing stories of early staff members who played such amazing roles and their dedication to getting SMR off and running.

No other person could have written SMR history other than Bob Ruesch.
—Jerry Donner, SMR Summer Staff, 1975–1977, and
Vice President of Group Sales from 2001 to 2006

To all the staff who worked and volunteered at Snow Mountain Ranch and who, over the years, were willing to labor, play, and create memories for others and themselves. Also, Barbara, who should have been a part of this story but is now. To Jennifer, my daughter, SMR was a good start for your life. Finally, and most importantly, to our Lord, who knew before the time of my time about Snow Mountain Ranch.

Contents

Introduction 9

In the Beginning 11
    Estes to Granby 1966 13
    A Job Offer 19
    Lessons Found on Muddy Roads 25
    Pinewood Lodge Room 101 31
    Arriving at Snow Mountain Ranch in March 1971 ... 35
    Granby Market Receipt Book 39
    Dick Engle Stories 41

Summer Stories 47
    The Summers of the Seventies 49
    First Staff 55
    The Building of Cabins, the Construction of Lodges ... 61
    Gary and Coffee Cups 67
    Hiring Summer Staff 71
    Missing Child 77
    Cutting Firewood 83
    Whispering Pines Chapel 87
    Summer Staff Musical, 1981 93
    The Chaplain's Kit 97
    The Doctor and the Mechanic 101
    Summer Campfires 107

Fall Solstice 111
    Fall Colors 113
    Weather and Alone Time 119
    First Snow 123

Winter Activities 127
    Opening Day of Ski Season...................................129
    Plowing Snow 131
    Group Arrivals: Nighttime 135
    Group Departures: Not Happening 139
    A Silent Journey..143
    Rescue and the National Guard 145
    Flanagan's Ski Shop..149
    Blizzard Driving..155
    A Winter's Sleigh Ride 161
    Pinewood Christmas Tree.......................................167
    The Day after Christmas..171
    Snow Slide at the Roller Rink 175

Just Ranch Stories..181
    Birthday with Rudy 183
    Deer Meat on the Table..187
    Four Clarabelle Stories 191
    The Bobcat and Clarabelle.....................................193
    Coyotes, Clarabelle, and a Rifle.............................195
    Mountain Man Caught in a Trap 197
    "So I Married Her" 199
    Rudy and Clarabelle Programs 201
    Great Spirit Poem 207
    Just Ranch Today, 2017 209

Final Thoughts...215

Introduction

Every book, each memory, every story starts with a beginning, and some stories never end, although they may change a little or a bit or some over time. This book contains the start of a "camp" that would be built board by board, nail by nail. Built on a dream, with a vision, even a whim or two, Snow Mountain Ranch YMCA began in the minds of a few of the YMCA of the Rockies Board members in the 1960s. Estes Park Center YMCA was not going to be able to gain any acreage. The accommodations at Estes Park were not built to the fullest, but it was time for growth. A different type of YMCA camp was envisioned as a place to branch out, a new facility, cabins, campgrounds, lodges, land to roam. There were mountains to climb, rivers to explore, and new families who would appreciate a facility similar in philosophy but unique in design. It was time to seek, search, research, and decide where something new could be created.

Thus, Snow Mountain Ranch was starting to evolve. A search for land began. Like the gold miners of the 1800s, several board members and staff searched for property across Colorado. The search was frustrating at times; promising as land looked on paper, it wasn't so in reality.

From land on the East Slope to acreage on the West Slope of the Colorado Rockies, trips were taken, possibilities considered, and persistence was always present.

Finally, after thinking every conceivable rock in the little state of Colorado was turned over in the land search, a realtor suggested looking at property in Grand County on the Western Slope. Close to a ski area, in a valley, a homestead called Just Ranch was for sale. Perhaps this was the right piece of land; maybe the quest in one way was close to an end. Perhaps, just perhaps, the search was over.

A trip with a few Y Board members was arranged, and a destination was set to look at a homestead on the Western Slope with the possibility of other land being purchased at the same time.

From the start of the journey, it is told, the anticipation was electric as the board members and Walt Ruesch drove to Grand County over Berthoud Pass, down the mountain, past the ski area, through Tabernash, and to Just Ranch to look at the Colorado homestead.

This land was the home of Rudy Just, his mother, Della Just, and Rudy's wife, Clarabelle. The homestead was home to sheep, horses, chickens, and history on every wall of the pioneer log house. More than a home, more than walls, windows, a roof, and a view of the Continental Divide, this was a place of generations where a family labored on land that was an unforgiving paradise, a small slice of heaven. They were the caretakers, stewards of the earth, their livestock, and each other, and watched out for their neighbors, even though they could not see the next house.

Here is the finalization of one story. The changing of Just Ranch, but the legacy left by the Just family, a ranch to be enjoyed by families, youth groups, conferences. There will be summer and winter adventures and the opportunity for children with medical issues to experience a week as campers.

Here is the beginning of lifetime memories, celebrating fifty years in 2019 of family commitment with staff willing to work to create a life of memories.

Then let us begin.

In the Beginning

Estes to Granby 1966

Therefore, as we have opportunity, let us do good to all people, especially to those who belong to the family of believers.
—Galatians 6:10

Many excursions were scheduled for groups to travel to Snow Mountain Ranch to catch the vision and scope of the future camp. Here, Walt Ruesch shares with the YMCA Board of Director's thoughts on what the future brings.

Every day you are at the Estes Park Center YMCA gas station, you can expect each day to be different. One day you might wash a commercial bus, another change tires. Sometimes the day is filled with cleaning windows, filling gas tanks, and answering questions about almost any subject that a guest might have.

This particular day started out as usual. Unlock the station, turn on the gas pumps, sweep the area around the gas pumps. You would fill the window wash bucket with water and get the windshield cloths ready for their assigned task. You tried to get all the chores completed before you opened. That rarely happened. Cars were thirsty, and drivers wanted to get started early on the family choice of rides, hikes, and shopping.

In all the preparation work, you also needed to recount the cash box, which you did at the Ad Building desk, but a second time would not hurt.

The day progressed as usual, gas-filling, window-washing, fix-a-flat day. Then Wendel Ley, a Y Board member, drove up in his Cadillac. I filled the thirsty beast, cleaned the expanse of windows, and offered to sweep out the rugs. Wendel wanted to talk, and for me that was unusual. "I was wondering if you could get tomorrow off," he said. "I need a driver for my car from here to a town on the West Slope and back again. You would be gone all day. Could you drive my car?" I was thinking, "Drive a Cadillac for a day in the Colorado Rockies, though Rocky Mountain National Park? What could be better?"

It seemed Wendel and the Y Board were on a road trip to Just Ranch, outside of Granby, to look at the homestead and make a decision about this piece of Colorado heaven being purchased for a new YMCA camp. I was to be the driver to board members.

There are times in a person's life that are milestones. Some people recall weddings, births of children, and national and international events as a landmark. The day was to become such a day for me, and little did I know or realize God's hand on this day and in the future and how my life was planned.

"Sure, I can get the day off," I said. After all, one of the gas station crew owed me a shift, problem solved.

The trip from Estes to Granby was one of me being the designated driver with Wendel explaining to the board passengers the opportunity, the future for the YMCA, and the possibility of the impact of families coming to another slice of heaven in Colorado, called Just Ranch.

I listened as Wendel outlined the day. It was as God had orchestrated the day with perfect July weather. The drive was the prelude to the symphony of the day, the time at Just Ranch the central piece, and then the ride home a final chorus.

We arrived in caravan driving down a rural, not-well-maintained dirt road, weaving in between ruts (Cadillacs sit low), and all I needed to do was take off a muffler or oil pan. Lunch was served as in most outings; there were sack lunches, but at a higher level, after all, this was the Y Board.

The members of the Y Board toured much of the property, with Wendel and Dwight Dannen answering question after question.

Finally, in the afternoon, we drove into the main homestead of Just Ranch where Della, Rudy, and Clarabelle made a living raising sheep and cattle and cutting hay.

The view of the valley to Indian Peaks was like a painting of spectacular quality. However, no artist could do such a scene justice. How to convey the beauty of God's continued masterpiece of creation taking the attractiveness of one visual form to another required God-given skills.

Author (on the gate with 8mm camera) and a board member, Jim Eggleston, looking back at the Just Homestead.
(Photo courtesy of Wendel Ley)

The members of the Board stood and looked in awe. We were standing at a place of ranch production that had been homesteaded for many decades. The land and the YMCA Board of Directors was now at a junction of human decision. One way was a loss of homestead identity, and yet another avenue was an opportunity for more than a family, yet many families, to experience the intricate and pure beauty of God's creation. The summer, this summer would change direction for many—the Just family, the corporate structure of the YMCA, and the opportunity for families and conferences to relax, vacation, and work in a place of tranquil beauty steeped in history. Not only a history of a homestead carved out of the valley by a ranch family that filled their house with memories, but also now a chance to change direction for more than one family, for a multitude of people, summer staff, conference, and families to create a lifetime of memories. I sensed this was a moment in time that would be a landmark moment, not only for the Just family or the YMCA, but for me as I was here for a reason, and that reason was not just to drive a Cadillac across a mountain range.

The Board gathered in the meadow between the log homestead and the livestock pens. You could sense a feeling of anticipation as they grouped together with a view of the Indian Peaks, the valley stretching to the mountains. A quiet wind whispered in some ways, "It is time, decide." I stood away, but close enough so I could hear the conversation from the board president.

He spoke but a few minutes about the amount of land that was available, the opportunity for the future, the cost, and finally about God's direction and directive of being here at this moment. There was a pause. "As we stand here, looking at what we can accomplish in the future, I would like to poll the board and see if we are in agreement to purchase this land." The moment of decision, commitment for generations was here. This was not official; the recorded vote would come later, but this moment was the vote of promise. "What is your pleasure, gentlemen? Raise your hands if you believe we should proceed with the purchase of this land." I watched as all hands went up, a vote of a collective commitment, now bonded together for the future.

Rudy and Clarabelle stood away from the Y Board, watching and seeing the expression of commitment. Rudy didn't say a lot, but his stature often spoke louder than words. As he witnessed the visual consensus, he placed his arm around Clarabelle, standing a bit taller. His smile was broad as the valley and as bright as the afternoon sun. Clarabelle looked up at him, smiling too. The torch was being passed. The land preserved for generations. The Just Homestead would not be carved up but designed with trails, cabins, lodges for generation after generation to come and enjoy.

The Y Board was in agreement; the Justs supported the decision. It was a defining moment. I was blessed to be a quiet part of the redirection of land that was loved, cared for, and used to sustain a family. Now the property would be loved by many families, cared for by other individuals, and available for decades of memories for many to enjoy.

Rudy and Clarabelle joined the Board for a moment. You could see pride and understanding from this moment on. The Just Homestead was going to be forever changed.

Goodbyes were said; promises to see each again soon were made. The Board gathered in their respective transportation for the ride back to Estes Park. Wendel and my passengers were quiet as we traveled back to Estes Park YMCA. We had all experienced a change, not only for the land of promise now, but a difference in our being. The board was now becoming the trustees of a future, set at their feet, agreed upon by humankind, and orchestrated by our Lord.

Snow Mountain Ranch had just begun.

A Job Offer

For I know the plans I have for you, declares the LORD, *plans to prosper you and not to harm you, plans to give you hope and a future. Then you will call on me and come and pray to me, and I will listen to you. You will seek me and find me when you seek me with all your heart.*
—Jerimiah 29:11–13

A person or group needs to know where the property entrance is. This rock-built rough-hewed sign was constructed in 1969.

In God's world, there are no consequences, and sometimes you think you fall into an unplanned adventure or perhaps a life-changing opportunity. In a jumbled world, an opportunity from God can appear, but it has to be recognized.

After a few years of working in the world of radio and television, which included a new entertainment venue called cable TV, I was ready for a change of job and scenery in that order. I wanted to return to Colorado, the place I felt more at home than anywhere else.

I figured I could stay with my parents for a few weeks in Denver, look for an exciting job in a top TV market, and have a career in the Mile High State. That was my thinking. Reality became more apparent and evident with each rejected job application. There was the standard remark of, "Thank you for coming in. We will be in touch," which meant, "Move on. We don't have work for you. That can be a real ego deflation factor to someone who was thinking he was the next local television anchorman.

My plan wasn't working out well for me. After weeks of searching and interviewing, it was evident an alternative solution needed to be crafted if I was to have a job and income anytime soon. My schedule was wide open and empty. There were no job interviews. The days were empty, somewhat like my checking account.

Living at home was okay with me, but my parents had not had another appetite in the house or car in the driveway for several years. Looking back at that time at home, I see now where a son returning to live in the house he grew up in could be cause for concern. Now with no job and less employment prospects, the situation was starting to look like I was becoming a permanent resident, at least to them.

One night, during dinner, Dad asked if I would like to go see the progress at the new camp, Snow Mountain Ranch. I thought that was a good idea. It would give us windshield time, although we hardly talked, and I had no job appointments, interviews, or applications to fill out. The day was completely open. The next morning, we were off on an adventure, at least for me.

Here is where prayer, trusting in God, doing His will, and understanding would present challenging opportunities each day and would be addressed.

The time at SMR was the usual meetings that were the purpose of the trip. It was accented with lunch and a few more directions given to staff as was always the case. With all the meetings completed as planned, we started the trip back home. Again, not a lot of talking except for the question of what I thought of the new camp.

A few days later, Dad asked if I would be interested in working at Snow Mountain Ranch. I would be doing family programs and anything else required that needed to be done. But before I said anything, he suggested another journey to Estes Park and to talk to a staff member about the working structure of a son working for his father.

He suggested while at Estes I talk to Dr. David Zimmerman. David and I discussed the job within the YMCA of the Rockies, my position as the son of the manager, and possible job description for SMR. That conversation lasted well over two hours as Dave and myself looked at all the facts, challenges, opportunities, danger zones of working at SMR with the knowledge the staff would know I was "manager's son."

Dr. David Zimmerman was a person of insightful questions that require answers with a depth of thinking and a whole lot of personal introspection and honesty. We talked for several hours on many subjects, including the YMCA, growing up as manager's son, how the family relationship would affect my job at SMR. If I took the job offer, would this be a career move? Or would this job just be a layover until something else came along? After a few hours of questions and answers, which produced more issues not only from him but from me, I was exhausted and understood the deeper meaning of interrogation, but in a good way.

Now, I had more questions than answers. I also had clearer thinking of what would be involved working for my father, even with a level of management between father and son. The job would have challenges as there was not a clear job description of exactly what I was responsible for.

On the way home each of us was in our own world. I was contemplating the conversation I had with Dr. Zimmerman, and I was also discussing the pros and cons with myself as what was best not only for me but also for Snow Mountain Ranch. I knew I needed to look at and answer the questions about working with my father and how that would affect a relationship with Dick Engle, who would be my direct supervisor.

I never saw my father play poker, and I never did play the game, but I knew enough of the game to know Dad had a poker face with very few tells. At least none that I ever could pick up on, and today was another one of those poker faces, keep quiet until the other person says something. I lost that round as we pulled into the driveway at our home.

"I think I would like to give the job at the camp a try," I said. "But I don't want it to be just a job. I want to make it more than that, a career." Dad sat quietly in the car, with his poker face look as he stared out the windshield. "Well then, you probably need to move up to Granby as soon as you can. The weekend would be a good time." Today was Thursday, and it wasn't like I had a lot to pack. The weekend it was then.

"Why don't you bring your car downtown to the Denver office [the YMCA of the Rockies at that time had an office in the YMCA in downtown Denver for the winter months] tomorrow, and I will get new tires on it as it looks like you could use them," Dad stated. I realized almost bald was an issue, and tires with traction for a vehicle in snow country was a necessity.

Things happen for a reason. In one moment you can be riding high and the next skidding on the path of life receiving severe emotional road rash. I was at a juncture, a choice, an opportunity to choose several directions. The offer at Snow Mountain Ranch was not by chance but, I believe, through God's will, and the fact I listened to His will and followed His direction was the choice that God intended I make.

I don't believe there was any favoritism involved. I was there, and the ranch needed another person who could create and administer programs, which included working with groups, and "any other task that is assigned." I was in the right place at the perfect time because God placed me there.

The choice of working for my father was addressed, challenged, joked about, and even cried over at times. But there was a cardinal rule that Dad and I discussed and agreed upon. We kept the covenant for as many years as I was at SMR, even after he retired, and

I was there one more year. We would discuss business in a business setting only, never at their home. I would keep the confidence of my work as to support and honor those whom I worked with and for. That was the rule and understanding. Never was I asked about work details at home; that was family time.

Dave Zimmerman and I had discussed that significant detail at length during our session as I was planning my life and a new career. Over the years, I was offered strong Christian council. Some of the direction I paid attention to; some I did not. When I didn't acknowledge a suggestion, like for so many in life, I wished I had.

From a difficult decision to come home to a life-changing opportunity for a career, it became a gift from God that I listened to and am forever grateful that I followed His direction.

Lessons Found on Muddy Roads

I give you sound learning, so do not forsake my teaching.
—Proverbs 4:2

The road is dry in this photo, but this is an excellent example of the entrance road leading to Pinewood Lodge. There was room to the right to plow snow during the winter. (Photo courtesy of Jane Morgan-Bost, SMR's first woman hike master for SMR.)

There is a classic movie titled *The Wild, Wild West*. In one scene an actor is seen sloshing through the muddy streets, with each step accumulating more mud on his gooey boots. In the beginning, the road into Snow Mountain Ranch was like that during the spring thaw. That is when I arrived for my new job in March of 1971. My Volkswagen Squareback, an ever-reliable car which contained most of my earthly belongings, turned off of US 40 and into a road, perhaps better described as a ribbon of mud and ruts. This road had the potential to capture a vehicle in the mire.

Welcome, welcome to living in Grand County. At that time a county with only one stoplight that I could find and with an abundance of muddy roads with one paved highway to my destination. I was home if I didn't get stuck.

Learning to drive on roads in the spring that are frozen wheel troughs in the morning and mud bogs in the afternoon is a rapid learning process. If you are not a good student and don't learn fast, you will be either breaking your steering suspension by trying to get out of a frozen rut or walking in the mud because you were driving too slow for the conditions. I decided to be an A student, thinking, "This too shall pass," only to be reminded spring comes each year.

Morning drives on rutted mud roads consisted of finding the proper width for your tires in the frozen mud and letting the substantial part of nature take its course. Trying to jump out of a rut to another would be sure to break the bead on your tire. The least of which alignment of the front axle was going to be needed. One never appreciates the relatively smooth surface of a paved highway until you have experienced frozen mud troughs on a rural road. Four-wheel drives were invented for such a time as this.

On the other hand, driving in the brown glue-like substance required another determined set of skills and goal setting. First, you never should stop. If you do, you are done. Your journey is over. Here is where you will stay overnight, captured, and frozen in the concrete brown mud, which is the best way to describe the predicament of your car. So you step (tromp) on the gas in my case (remember a VW

Squareback) and go to the determined destination, never relinquishing the inertia and physics of forwarding motion.

And this brings up another part of the issue, the approaching vehicle. That driver is doing the same thing, a new form of "chicken" is now in play. Here are the rules. If you are more significant than the approaching vehicle, you can probably move over a bit and continue. If you are smaller, you must stay the course. If the dirty stuff is flying about, get the windshield washer and wipers going ahead of time because you will be baptized, partially blinded, and caked in brown. If you can stop (four-wheel drives and brave souls only), do so and let the other vehicle figure out what to do. If both of you stay and greet each other, you can have a conversation to catch up and share information about the rest of the road.

In my VW case, I continued to forge ahead, hands gripping the wheel in the best white-knuckle fashion in the lowest gear and the motor RPMs close to the red line on the tachometer as possible. I would wave with one hand for a second as we passed. Then the inevitable would happen.

Splat, smash, the mud from the other vehicle would grace the design of my low-riding, underpowered, once-robin's-egg-blue car. It would sound like meteorites smashing into the exterior of the vehicle. The windshield would be mud-covered brown, and the road in front of you obscured.

At this point of your muddy mission, the goal is to just get to your destination. You are hoping you remember what lies ahead because you cannot quite see where you are heading. Windshield wipers were never designed for mud removal. The washing fluid is for other gooey objects such as bugs and light dirt, not a full earthly assault of gooey earth.

Finally, with your faster-beating heart, you pass the vehicle coming your way. That part of the mud war is over, and you travel on to your destination, only to know that in the not-too-distant future you will again have the opportunity to repeat your travels again down the soupy highway of driving life.

What I learned from spring driving in the Rocky Mountains is a lesson in life—that determination and destination sometimes are in concert with each other. I decided to turn off the secure path, and that will bring you challenges that are not the easiest or often not the cleanest route, but in many cases the most fulfilling path you can travel.

After the mudslinging, sliding, slipping, and wondering what I had done to myself and my vehicle, Pinewood Lodge, with its A-frame lobby design, came into view. It indeed was not the rainbow and the pot of gold, but the parking lot was not a treacherous mess of mud either. Although my car was bleeding liquid dirt, I didn't care. I didn't have to slosh my way in and through it.

I turned the engine off. It was quiet, no traffic sounds, only the wind moving through the pine trees and the branches keeping sway with the whim of the breeze. I looked around. The scenery was pristine. The deep blue of the Colorado sky was candy to my sight. Here, in the high altitude of the Colorado Rockies was the beginning of a family resort, a conference center. A place for college students to come, work, play, and create memories. What was a homestead with Mile High pioneers working for a living for many years now was given over to a new brand of a pioneer. Staff, families, and conferences, learning to live, whether on vacation or here to learn as an attendee at a seminar or staff supporting the two, you automatically became part of a new direction of homesteading.

I sensed not only a new beginning for me but for the people who came here to Snow Mountain Ranch. The place imprinted on you that this property, this former homestead land was unique in so many ways. Like every turn on a hiking trail, there is a new adventure, experience, and feeling that awaited you.

Sitting in the convenience of a vehicle was no more. I opened the door, stepped out, and felt the brisk air of high country in Colorado. Over the coming years, I sense arriving staff and guests have similar feelings. You have reached your destination, but your journey was just beginning.

Opening the door to Pinewood Lodge, stepping into the lobby, seeing the height of the A-frame design only confirmed my feeling. The journey was beginning. My new home was going to be just down the hall.

Pinewood Lodge Room 101

This is how we know that we belong to the truth and how we set our hearts at rest in his presence.
—1 John 3:19

Pinewood Lodge, 1972, notice the trees left in the parking lot. During the spring, this parking lot was extremely muddy, keeping housekeeping busy with continually cleaning the lobby.

Sometimes housing is not what you expect. It can be better, worse, or merely enjoyable. My new home, Pinewood 101, was not what I expected.

Sure, there was a bathroom, a bed, and a small desk. It was my space, my place, my room, my home in the Colorado Rockies. My area before there was something in social media called Myspace.

I looked around the room which was on the bottom floor of the lodge. I was next to an outside door and across from housekeeping storage. I had two inside and two outer walls, a large window, and a comfortable, safe place to sleep. You could have not asked for more. God had provided a home, a new job, a start to a different chapter in my life.

I closed the door to my room, which, for me, signaled the completion of a journey and the start of another. When God closes a door, generally, He opens another for you to pass through. Sometimes He wants you to wait in the hallway. I wondered if He was going to be waiting in His hallway, or would I go through another door and if that was part of His plan for my life.

The walls of the room were a kind of blond paneling, which was in style in the 1970s. There was no artwork on the walls, and I was told there would be none that could be placed on the walls. Photo frames were set in windowsills or top of shelves. That was the only option. I didn't have that many pictures I wanted to display. After all, who would see them, except for me.

The view from my curtained windows was of trees, lots of trees. Snow Mountain Ranch was in a lodgepole forest that stretched for mile upon mile. You could not see Pinewood Lodge until you were almost upon the structure. To say there was an abundance of firewood was an understatement. But being in a forest, thick with trees, also gave way to disorientation at times.

One of the benefits of having your domicile in Pinewood 101 was the commute to work. Out your door, turn left, walk down the hall, turn right, climb up the stairs, and you are at the administrative offices of Snow Mountain Ranch. I considered showing up at work sometimes in my pajamas but squelched the thought quickly, although the temptation remained for the time I lived in Pinewood, especially on days I thought I might be running late to work.

It is hard to be late to work, as you were on call most of the time. Early days and late nights dictated a schedule, and services for conferences and guests dictated what the work schedule was to be. It seems about the time you wanted to rest or sleep, a conference group pulled into the parking lot. For some reason, the leader wanted the kids to get in their rooms for the remainder of the night.

For all the convenience of the room, because of the comfort of a new domicile, I felt blessed, safe, and at home. This was home for me now. As I looked at the few boxes I had, the clothes hanging, the desk with my few books and writing paper, I could see the trappings of a place of refuge. The sounds of the lodge would take some getting used to. The noise of groups and guests would, no doubt, also be in that category. That was lodge living. That was where I was granted a place to sleep, rest, relax, and call home.

Arriving at Snow Mountain Ranch in March 1971

For I know the plans I have for you, declares the LORD, plans to prosper you and not to harm you, plans to give you hope and a future.
—Jeremiah 29:11–13

Jerry Donner worked at SMR starting in 1975 with the Program Department. However, one of his first assignment was to help ready a new lodge for guests. During his YMCA career, he became the Estes Park Conference Director for in 1981 and Managing Director of Snow Mountain Ranch in 1985. He was promoted to Group Sales Director for Estes Park and Snow Mountain Ranch in 1988. He kept this photo behind his desk and would refer to it when asked how he achieved his current job status. Jerry retired in 2006 as Vice President of Membership and Sales. (Photo, Donner collection.)

Perhaps to start at the beginning is best. Back in Indiana, I was a young adult wanting to return to my roots in Colorado, where I was raised. I knew it was time to go back to the Mile High State, find work, and live where I believe I belong.

Where would I work? What would I do was not thoroughly thought out, but trusting God's direction was what I desired to do. I had resigned from the local TV cable station and packed up my loyal VW Squareback car. I headed west, leaving behind the memories of the Hoosier State and striking out to a new adventure. With an unknown career or job, and with a depleting checking account, what could possibly be wrong with such a plan?

God always has a plan for our lives. We have our plans, and God has His plans as well for our lives.

At the end of the conversation with Dr. Dave, I could see that working at Snow Mountain Ranch was a predestined gift from God. One offered and accepted by a young man willing to trust God, follow His will, and carve a career in the uncharted corporate territory for the YMCA of the Rockies at Snow Mountain Ranch.

On the ride back to my parents' home, Dad and I talked about the job, the challenges (with him, there were no challenges, only opportunities), and how I would fit in. I never considered I would not be accepted or fail. God was in charge, in control. I would give the job my best, my all.

So I journeyed to a county with no stoplights, thousands of square miles of ranch and recreation, where you left your doors unlocked, keys in your car, and in many cases, everyone knew your name.

This work journey began with no presuppositions of what the work would be like, nothing of a hidden agenda from me or others, just a guy on a new adventure crafted by God.

The route to Snow Mountain Ranch was over Berthoud Pass, down into Middle Park, Winter Park, Frasier, and Tabernash. I arrived at the ranch midafternoon. I was ready for a new chapter in my young life. This portion of my life that would span a dozen years. At times that took a path of challenge, heartache, unbridled joy, exploration, and an opportunity to grow and learn and appreciate life in a way never imagined. I was about to be blessed in some ways I would recognize and other ways not so evident.

Pinewood Lodge is designed as a large A frame with two wings making up rooms, a commercial kitchen, meeting rooms, and dorm space. It is the first building you see that tells you, you have arrived at your destination.

The road to the lodge was the perfect mud storm of a rutted way. Once you started, you didn't stop until you needed to. Spring in the Colorado Rockies created a thawing process during the day from the snow and freezing at night because of the low temperatures.

Dick Engle, camp director, was in his office. We talked for a few minutes with welcoming statements. "I think you might like to get settled in your room." I followed him to my new home.

"This is your room, Pinewood 101," Dick said with a flourish as he opened the door to my new home. There was a double bed, private bath, small sink, and, as a bonus, a refrigerator! I looked at the fridge and wondered if I was to create my own meals. Dick sensed my thought and stated the appliance was there for my personal needs and dinner was upstairs at five, about three hours away. He handed me a key and closed the door. I was home. I had a master key to the ranch, a place to stay and dinner on the calendar.

Unpacking didn't take too long, how much can you place in a VW Squareback? What I believed I didn't need was in "storage" in Denver at my parents' house.

My first "job" came before dinner that evening. The road that led to Pinewood Lodge and the Administration Building was a consistency of clay and mud, in which much had taken up residence in my wheel wells. "I would clean those out—it will freeze tonight, and you won't be able to drive your car till spring," sated Don Hay, who oversaw construction and was the self-appointed head of the mud police. I had not thought that mud would be a big issue. Until you are tasked with the chore of cleaning out your mud-encased wheel wells, you have little or no idea how much brown, cold, sticky, messy mud you have in the wheel wells of your vehicle. Then you are blessed with the opportunity to do that muddy chore. I finished just as it was getting dark and almost time for dinner.

My arms were caked in dirt, my clean jeans a thing of the past. My attitude, grateful, but weary, and thankful for the advice. I drove the car to keep the wheels free as the road was now partially frozen. I now had a car that was useable because of a caring person offering a city boy rural mountain advice. I learned to rely on Don over the years for honest, caring, loving guidance and support.

After dinner, I went back to my room, the lodge empty except for me. All other staff—the few that were there—lived in additional housing away from the lodge.

I listened to the sounds of an empty building. I wandered the echoing halls. I sat in the expanse of the lobby, hearing my thoughts and heartbeat and the rhythm of the lodge. I thought about arriving here, starting a new career. I listened to the gentle chill of the wind, as I trusted more on our Lord than I ever had before. For the next day, a new adventure awaited.

Tomorrow would be a new start, a beginning of a new job, but for now, all of Pinewood Lodge was my home with my comfortable, cozy, small room. This was my private lodge real estate.

Finally, I went to my room, closed my door, and slept the first night in my new home.

Granby Market Receipt Book

You must have accurate and honest weights and measures, so that you may live long in the land the LORD your God is giving you.
—Deuteronomy 25:15

    Moving to a small rural mountain town takes some getting used to. Things are different than in a city or in a metro area. People in a small town have a different rhythm to life. Coffee shops are filled in the morning with a verbal town newspaper from the coffee club which churned out facts, memories, and plans at the speed of sound.

    If you need to see someone, you can drive to the town generally in the morning, and you have a good chance of locating them at the local Sip & Chat Café. Cell phones, pagers were not invented in the 1970s—phone calls were on landlines, usually four people to a circuit.

    Household supplies were at the hardware store or the local market. If the store didn't have it, you probably didn't need it. If you required a specific item, either you drove to the "big city" over the Continental Divide or waited until the local store could order it for you.

    Clothes in the area were purchased at the Granby Trading Post. You had to like the cut of ranch-style clothes. That is what they had; that is what you wore. The best selection of cowboy hats was available along with multiple designs in shirts (Wrangler and Lee), working jeans, and "go to church" gloves. All in all, everything you required was in town. You would go from store to store to get the supplies, clothing, and food you need.

    The first time I went to Don's Market, the local grocery store in Granby, I traveled back in time. In an era where practical was placed ahead of glittering displays. There was sawdust on the butcher shop the floor and shelves filled with the familiar substances of nutrition. Absent was a sushi bar and gourmet deli. Present were the meat, cheeses, coffee, and nutritional needs for the day.

There was a single drawer for the cash register, and the cost of items was memorized by the staff and run up on the button machine. When presented with the bill, there were two choices, cash or sign a receipt book with your name on the spine to be paid at the end of the month.

I had never seen a system like this before, a receipt book procedure of accounting. The rancher in front of me got the tally of his bill. The livestock feed had been loaded into his truck, groceries bagged (in paper bags, the only choice), and the total purchase amount announced. "Put it in the book," he said, and the cashier pulled out a drawer full of receipt books, found his last name, wrote the total down on one of the pages, of which I noticed the book was almost filled, and placed the receipt book back in its proper place.

The rancher grabbed the multiple sacks of groceries. How he could carry that many bags was beyond me, and he walked out to his truck.

I was tallied up, fewer bags, no livestock feed, and told what I owed. I had cash, a checkbook, and an opportunity to learn about the receipt book system. "Can I put it in the book?" I asked. The credit check was a simple one. "Who are you, where do you work, what do you do, are you planning on staying here in Middle Park, and where are you living?" I signed off on the purchase, took my few bags of groceries, and walked to my car.

I was now a little more part of the community. I had credit at the local grocery. Credit approval came in an instant with a look, handshake, and a promise to cover my bill each month. The way you took care of your monthly bill was to come in and pay in person. No invoice was sent out; it was a time-tested honor system. It was small-town life, significant responsibility to the community, opportunity to grow. I was thankful for the trust and the welcoming into a community by the simple process of a grocery receipt book.

Dick Engle Stories

*So give your servant a discerning heart to govern your
people and to distinguish between right and wrong.*
—1 Kings 3:9

*With the continual need to "push dirt," Dick would take
a part of his day to assist the construction crews.*

Richard and Sylvia Engle arrived at Snow Mountain Ranch in the spring of 1970. Dick, as the staff called him, met Sylvia at Estes Park Center when they were both on summer staff, Dick in 1957 and both in 1958. So it was a natural progression when the family was on vacation at Estes Park area, camping with their two daughters to talk to Walt, the managing director of Estes Park, about memories of their time working at Estes Park Center during the summer.

As conversations go, the subject of working for the YMCA of the Rockies came up, and Walt mentioned the new camp on the Western Slope, Snow Mountain Ranch, and perhaps they should look at working there as the director of the new camp. As they say, after a visit and a look at the property, the rest is history. Dick packed up the family and moved to the Colorado Rockies to continue his career in the YMCA. Life would never be the same for this Texas family. Colorado living does that to you.

When Dick first arrived at work in August of 1970, there were no paved roads, and would not be for several years. A private phone line was not even offered in rural Grand County at that time. "When we arrived at Snow Mountain Ranch, we wondered where we would sleep as the trailer we would live in was not ready," stated Dick. A room was readied at Pinewood Lodge for their first night. Sylvia recalled that she felt they had died and gone to heaven. "It [SMR] was a beautiful untamed land," Dick remembered of when he arrived at his new job. Their two children, Cindy and Patrice, were seven and four years old. Both graduated from high school in Grand County. Life would be completely different with new challenges not experienced or found in the metropolitan areas of Oklahoma.

There are many memories of working with Dick, but only a few could be addressed here. Another complete book could be written about his and Sylvia's dedication to creating a memorable family and conference experience. So here are a few memories of working with Dick.

Because there was continued construction, occasionally Dick would have time to help in the grading of roads or the moving of dirt. During the slow time in the spring, Dick felt the tubing hill needed to be groomed and be in better shape for the next winter activities, which he accomplished. That was the easy part and was completed in a short amount of time. Then the fun began as Dick decided that breaching or crossing the water-filled irrigation ditch was a good idea. After all, the dozer could do that task efficiently.

What needed to happen was to get the John Deere, Johnny Popper as it was fondly named, to the other side of the ditch. With the water already running in the trench, there was the distinct possibility of mud at the bottom. Sometimes, thoughts run through your mind that you can do the impossible because the challenge is there. Getting a small bulldozer to the other side of a muddy, water-filled ditch should be a matter of just driving across. That was the thought and the plan.

What is perceived as easy and what would become a reality are many times at opposite ends of the scale, as this was the case. Dick found out that mud is by far more onerous than a dual-track, go-almost-anywhere dozer. He started across the ditch, proceeded to get stuck, and then decided to get unstuck by working his way out, and became mired in the mud. Dick was going nowhere, and the dozer was down for the murky, muddy count.

Getting a heavy machine unstuck takes a more massive device that isn't stuck, of which Snow Mountain Ranch did not own. However, one of the road construction companies did have such a machine. They were able to rescue the water-and-mud-trapped piece of metal from its muddy grave using a long heavy cable. Glenn Tilghman, who was essentially the maintenance department, was in charge of cleaning and repair of the water-soaked and mud-encased machine. Getting the mud and muck washed out and getting the dozer running again was no easy task. Dick went home for an extended, well-deserved shower. The day was over, the project accomplished, but the story of Dick and the irrigation ditch would continue.

Somehow a few canisters of a new product being used by local authorities called Mace was procured for the camp. I imagine the underlying reason to have this product as if there was an issue with a bear or other four-foot predator that had claws. In this case, enhanced pepper spray on steroids would be useful. There was a warning label on the canister clearly stating about the potential reaction from the spray. Nothing was said on any label about what happens when you spray this product in your VW bug with the windows rolled up, even if you aim for the back seat.

In the world of "I didn't know better," spraying Mace toward the back seat is something you only do once. Dick was traveling with another staff member toward the entrance of the camp on an errand run and decided to show this person how the Mace would spray from the canister. One small push of the actuator was enough to fill the car with the product as it dispersed in the air. Osmosis is a beautiful thing for perfume and scented candles, but not this product.

Watery eyes, coughing, and thinking it was not the best decision caused the two passengers to exit the moving vehicle and letting the car continue, with open doors and windows to stop on its own. When it did, it was on and in a snowbank.

Coughing and walking back to the lodge, Dick and the staff member called Glenn to come and retrieve the Maced VW and let the vehicle air out for a few days. However, the story does not end knowing that in the winter the VW seemed to be aired out from the Mace. Then the summer's warmth created round two of the Mace that had been sprayed that would once again bring tears to your eyes, of a memory of a winter incident. The car windows were left open for several days, just to be sure there was a clearing of the air.

Not afraid to wield a shovel, especially at a groundbreaking event, many of the staff and board members were always available to pitch in for the photo opp.

Dick loved to help when dirt needed to be moved, a ditch dug, or a load of lumber picked up and delivered to one of the many construction sites on grounds. We all would help where needed to further the construction schedule as cabins were rented on specific dates and lodges booked which meant they needed to be ready. Many times, getting a reprieve from office work was welcome.

You could become proficient in operating earth-moving machinery, driving dump trucks, and digging ditches with a backhoe. Dick became an accomplished operator of this type of machinery. Often you would find him working alongside other construction workers, moving dirt, leveling areas for parking, etc.

This was Dick's way. Whatever it took to get the work finished or the task accomplished, he would do. Many times, he would volunteer to drive to Denver for supplies stating that he was the most dispensable person. Paperwork could wait, but to prepare a cabin for an arrival of a vacationing family could not. When the delivery was made, Dick would change hats, put on the manager's cap, then complete what tasks were needed by staying in the office, sometimes late into the evening.

Sylvia supported Richard, as she always called him, knowing the ministry and mission required significant amounts of time sacrifice away from family. We all knew that was part of the package that was merely part of the privilege of being a piece of a far more meaningful picture than we all could imagine. We were Team SMR, striving to do the best, be the best, and have the best for staff, guests, and conference members.

Standards were set from the top and filtered down to others in the corporate structure. Dick set the standards high, the bar above average, close to excellent. But the bar was set with everyone being on the team.

Snow Mountain Ranch would not accomplish what growth it did during the time Dick was the manager without everyone rallying around the common goals of excellence. Dick worked hard, many times harder than others. He played just as hard too in skiing, softball, hiking with his wife, and helping his girls with their horses and participation in cross-country skiing.

For the years that Dick and Sylvia were at Snow Mountain Ranch, lives were touched. Just ask the staff whom he hired and worked with; they will tell you the rest of the story.

Summer Stories

The Summers of the Seventies

For I know the plans have for you, declares the LORD, *plans to prosper you and not to harm you, plans to give you hope and a future.*
—Jeremiah 29:11

The Snow Mountain management team, Richard Engle, Robert Ruesch and Walter Ruesch, 1972
(Photo, author's collection taken around 1972)

The seventies was unique as our nation was at that time. Snow Mountain Ranch was finding its own direction. The cost of gas was between $0.40 and $0.50 a gallon. New cars were on average around $2,700 for a "good ride."

Richard Nixon was president, then came along Gerald Ford and Jimmy Carter. The country experienced the resignation of one president and the end of a war in a land far, far away.

McDonald's fast food offered the $0.70 Quarter Pounder and a $0.35 shake. If you wanted coffee, that was $0.15, including refills.

Movies of note were *Star Wars, Jaws,* and *Kramer vs. Kramer. The French Connection* launched a whole new generation of movie style, as well as the *Poseidon Adventure.*

Disco was the place to be seen dancing in your leisure suit. Free love was found out not to be free, and the illegal use of marijuana was part of the enlightened seventies culture.

In all ways, the world still rotated the same way it had, and summer was a vacation for most college students. Tuition for college was around $3,000, and minimum wage, $1.60. Snow Mountain Ranch had opened on July 25, 1969, with little fanfare. As the kitchen dishwasher was not installed, dishes were scrubbed clean in one of Pinewood Lodges vacant rooms, the bathtub serving in a different capacity.

College students continued to seek summer work away from home and related to their major. Applications from the state and private schools were looked over. The first year's SMR summer staff were taken from the students that applied for Estes Park. One person was hired for Estes Park and upon arriving was asked if he would like to consider going to Snow Mountain to work for the summer. "Being a Georgia boy and having a curious personality, I said yes," stated Jim Scarr. "It was the best decision I could have made. Snow Mountain Ranch changed my life." This type of life-changing statement was heard many times that Snow Mountain was unique in its own way.

Carved from homestead land, held to tradition, and charged with making memories that would become a tradition, the property was perfect for creating a family/conference and staff center that would impact lives and create memories that last a lifetime.

So they came, summer staff from all walks of life, full-time staff, some transplanted from Estes Park and given the challenge to build something new. Summer staff invented new programs for day camp. Families were experiencing the start of a new trend called RV camping. Recreational vehicles were starting to hold their own form of a family experience. RV camping was becoming a vacation alternative for families.

Conferences that wanted a different conference style would book their venue at Snow Mountain Ranch. High Flight, Logos Bookstore, Choral Arts Seminar, and Village Missions were a few of the first groups at Snow Mountain Ranch.

All of this comfortable cauldron of activity was going on as was the continuing building of cabins, lodges, and conference gathering places. Summer staff stayed in the walkout basement of the roller rink.

Roads were built, and a county of ranchers and business owners talked about the new facility between Granby and Tabernash. The SMR staff was willing to give extra effort to make a family camp from a homestead. There was a feeling of doing something beyond the day and the summer. You were a part of a greater cause now and for the future.

Ski groups from Kansas, Nebraska, Oklahoma, Texas, and Colorado churches, along with YMCAs from the same states booked rooms and ski lessons for a week of challenging the laws of gravity and inertia at a ski area known as Winter Park, a park of Denver Mountain Parks. Many went home with "raccoon eyes" from ski goggles, and several others complemented the look with crutches from an ill-advised run down a slope that was beyond their athletic ability, but not past the bragging points and sympathy of friends, families, and peers.

The lure of the Winter Olympics added to the opportunity for Snow Mountain Ranch to grow at a fast rate. Even when the citizens of Colorado voted down the winter Olympics of 1976, that didn't slow the speed of construction. From 1970 to 1980 the occupancy of Snow Mountain went from 184 to 2,800. That was America then as it is now, thriving and growing.

The opportunity was there to create something out of a wilderness that was once land to the Native Americans and then for homesteaders. Pioneers dug a living by ranching, clearing fields rock by rock to grow and harvest summer hay for livestock.

Wagon wheel ruts of progress turned slowly before SMR became a reality. But change was inevitable as the only constant changes. Grand County, once a ranching community, was being invaded by a growing ski industry and summer tourism. President Dwight Eisenhower came to fish in the Frasier River in the 1950s. That put the town of Frasier and Grand County on the map as a possible place to explore. Eventually, the town of Frasier became known as the Icebox of the Nation because of the plummeting subzero winter temperatures. The snow-tire industry took advantage of that slogan, bragging on how good their snow tires performed even in the harsh conditions of Colorado winters.

A change was coming to Grand County, and Snow Mountain Ranch was a part of that change as more and more people discovered the pristine beauty of Middle Park with the vast views of the Colorado Rockies. The simple life of the small town was now becoming not as simple. There were no traffic jams unless two people stopped on the road to talk to each other.

There was one movie theater, a single grocery store, and a few gas stations and restaurants, now a rural ranch paradise changing as the discovery of God's incredible beauty was revealed as progress moved into the county.

It was a time that would change a quiet community into a year-round playground for America. Snow Mountain Ranch was to be a part of the charge, to be a positive change agent, and to become a supportive member of the community.

When Ty Woodward, a staff transplant from Estes Park Center, was tasked with helping build the first structures at Snow Mountain Ranch, he was also tasked with getting a business phone line, of which the same phone number is still in use. He recalls the story of talking to the local phone office of Mountain Bell and requesting a private business line. "There was a pause and then laughter," he stated. "The phone employee clearly stated that I could have a phone line, private, not a chance, but there was a good chance of only having three other people on the line!" It took only a few years before a private phone line was installed, but the process of becoming a business was starting, even when a four-person phone line, with a distinctive ring, was as good as you could expect at that time.

There was the pure happiness of being welcomed in a community that did not experience a lot of change but in the next decade would see an explosion of change.

I arrived to work full-time in March of 1971. My license plate for my VW was ZB-545, the number of cars registered in Grand County at that time.

I posted a letter the day I became an employee of Snow Mountain Ranch. The postage was twenty-five cents, and the postmaster now knew my name, where I was working, where I came from.

That was the small-town way.

First Staff

For the sake of my family and friends, I will say, "Peace be within you."
—Psalm 122:8

The first SMR staff started working at Estes Park
Center and then moved to the camp mid-June.

There are many individuals, and families that helped build, mold, and create Snow Mountain Ranch. Ty and Fern Woodward were one of the first families to live on the property. Ty was a do-anything, build-anything person, which was needed desperately in the beginning years. Also, there were Don and Edna Hay and their two sons. Don oversaw all building construction for many years. Each had a role, a precise and also a general part at the beginning of Snow Mountain Ranch. Without dedicated couples willing to go to a new place with unknown challenges, uproot a family, and build a vision, SMR would not have been what it has become.

Ty Woodward - and his wife Fern agreed to pull up stakes and move to SMR in 1967 to help open SMR. Ty was a carpenter, builder, maintenance person, an all-around fix-it person.

In construction, it is a known factor that where and how you place the footers and foundation will directly relate to the sound structure of the building. Planning and critical decision-making, including goal setting and with a bit of dreaming, was what was needed to accomplish a dream, including the teamwork of many.

In the summer of 1971, Glen and Judy Tilghman arrived at camp and became staff. Glen could fix anything that was mechanical, build what needed to be constructed, and continue to do this with a gracious smile. In the early years, Judy stayed home with their two sons, then was pressed into service in housekeeping for many years. To date, their employment at SMR is the longest of any employee.

Judy Tilghman - oversaw housekeeping for 30 plus years. This photo is representative of the amount of linen needed to be carried to the lodges and cabins each day.

Glen is and will continue to be a prankster. He lightened the load and lowered the stress of working with his humor, at least for all who were not a part of the prank! You knew something was going to happen if you were around him, and he had a particular grin on his face. Someone was going to be blessed by his thinking!

Gary Van Horn, food service director, had purchased a new avocado-colored vehicle. He was proud of the color and the car, which got Glen's attention, as what could be done to compliment Gary's new vehicle.

Paint codes are found on the inside panel of a car door; all you need to match the paint is the code, and you will have an exact color match. As vehicles are more often than not left unlocked, it was only a matter of Glen retrieving the paint code, ordering the paint, and finding a vehicle to bless with the same color as Gary's new, always-clean car.

There was a slightly old panel truck that was part of the housekeeping department. The paint scheme was ragged and rusty, to say the least. That poor, sad vehicle needed a good sanding and painting. Glen had just the color to endow new life to the truck. After all, if you lost the truck in the parking lot, the bright color would make it easier to find. The thought of painting the truck could have gone to the efficiency of housekeeping being able to locate their vehicle and return to work in a shorter time. The bright color would make it easier to find their mode of transportation. That was the idea, at least.

Glenn Tilghman - he and Judy signed on in 1971. Glenn more than likely pushed more dirt, built more roads, and maintained more vehicles than would ever be recorded.

The appointed day arrived, and Glen drove the newly painted, bright-colored truck to the parking lot where Gary's car was parked. There was a parking spot next to his shiny green vehicle. The newly painted truck was placed on display. Side by side, the two were a pair, like a four-wheeled version of Mutt and Jeff. Both clean, one racy and the other boxy.

After lunch Glen walked back to the maintenance barn, leaving staff to see the visual match. As luck would have it, the parking lot was not full, so the full impact of the two was not easily missed.

As for Gary's response to the matching color of his cherished vehicle, there was not a lot of reaction over the years from Gary. He took the prank in stride.

Because Glen was very knowledgeable in the mechanics of vehicles, the staff would naturally go to him to get a mediocre-running vehicle running correctly. This, many times, gave Glen the opportunity to mess with the mind of the car owner and the mechanical operation as well. Dick seemed to have breakdowns more than most people, and he would ask Glen for the favor of his expertise. Glen would always oblige and solve the problem. One time, however, Glen could not help himself; it was time to prank Dick. The beloved Ford two-door that he drove was having an issue with running rough. Glen looked at it, told Dick to wait a little bit, and he would have it "repaired" for him.

Dick picked up the repaired Ford and started to drive it back to the main lodge. As he drove his repaired car, there was smoke, lots of smoke coming from the exhaust. It was a car with a pollution mission to fog the world. Dick didn't notice anything for a few minutes, yet others saw and smelled the smoke-filled exhaust. Soon, Dick saw his trail of grey smoke and turned around to visit Glen with this new problem. Of course, it was repaired in a very brief amount of time, and Dick was on his way with no exhaust trail. Glen was a hero, a mechanical genius; he continues to be the vehicle whisperer of the valley.

Glen did eventually confess to the prank, but later. Listening to Glen recall the story, his laughter fills the room as he relates this tale of a vacuum line inserted into a can of oil, creating a memorable, smelly, visual prank.

When you live together on a property, work together, sometimes over eighteen hours a day, you get to know people at many levels. Because Glen and Judy were about keeping life light and fun, you could expect to be taken in on a prank at some point, when you least expected it.

All of Glen's pranks were in good fun and never harmful.

On the other side of Glen's humor was his depth of understanding and acceptance of life's circumstances. His compassion and love for each person he worked with, summer staff and full-time staff, would show in what he quietly had to say. His simple statements allowed a window of support at the exact time you needed that care.

When my father passed away, Glenn and Judy were present to offer what was needed. They provided a quiet moment, a compassionate look, a hug, or just an ear to listen. I was living in California at the time Dad became fatally ill with a heart attack. For several days his recovery never became a recovery. And then he was welcomed into heaven.

That following summer, I visited Glen and Judy at their home. The leaves of the aspen trees chanted their continued wind-driven song. We talked about the times we worked together. Not only the fun but the challenges we faced and were able to meet and solve.

As I was getting ready to take my leave, of which I remember I continued to put off as I didn't want the evening to end, Glen looked at me and talked about working with my dad and how much it meant to him and Judy. He paused and said, "Losing a parent isn't easy, the hurt will always be there, but each day, each year, there will be a little less hurt. It will never go away, but neither will the good memories, they will be there too forever."

The healing started at that moment from a mechanic who began to repair a sad heart, this time with words and not wrenches. That is Glen, a person who fixes things.

The Building of Cabins, the Construction of Lodges

Unless the L ORD *builds the house, the builders labor in vain.*
—Psalm 127

Cabins were constructed year around. This cabin was named Morning Star by its donors. Notice the door under the porch that is a donor's closet access. Every cabin donor is given a place to keep personal items.

The sound of hammers striking nails, the growl of saws cutting wood for walls, and the vibration of concrete trucks rumbling were everyday familiar sounds. SMR was in a frenzied building stage. Cabins and lodges were going up at the rate of the number of people hired for the construction crews.

The plan was to create a facility for families and conferences to enjoy all year long. The goal was to rough in as many cabins as possible, then when winter arrived you could work on the inside. The goal was not met all the time.

Roads needed to be completed to where a cabin or lodge construction was planned. Besides, the building of structures, the infrastructure of water, sewer, and electricity was met before the first load of lumber and concrete was ever delivered.

Glenn, the dirt mover and carver of roads. Each day he was working on a big, noisy equipment, staying just ahead of the construction crews by getting the site prepared for the building of what was planned for that piece of ground. You generally could locate where Glenn was working by listening for the diesel grader or dirt mover.

The next phase had the construction crews pouring the concrete footers and foundations for cabins which sprung up like wildflowers in the meadows. Glenn would have already moved on to the next area of the building process.

One bonus for fireplaces was the massive number of trees that were cut down because of construction. Every day more trees were felled for roads or structures. The summer staff wood crew was tasked with the job of cutting the fallen trees into lengths for burning in the lodge or cabin fireplaces at Estes Park and Snow Mountain Ranch. Several times I was "honored" with the opportunity, usually on my day off, to take a load of wood to Estes Park YMCA, over Trail Ridge. The vehicle I drove was a chronologically challenged and stacked high with firewood. The truck was a stick shift, noisy, slow, but mechanically sound. The trip was an ever-shifting challenge to make the ascent to the top of Trail Ridge, which is twelve thousand feet above sea level and change. There were over eleven miles of the road above timberline. To add to the challenge was being able to not continually look at God's masterpiece of a created splendor.

If you didn't go visit the construction site almost every day, you would be impressed at how fast cabins were being built. One day a foundation, a week later walls were up, and trusses for the roof were being hoisted and secured into place. Windows, furniture, and finally guests were next. It seemed like a cabin was just about finished, and it was rented. How reservations knew when to rent and not rent was directed from an authority higher than the staff building the cabin.

Conference lodges, Aspenbrook and Silver Sage, were designed for groups and families. The expansive two-story lobby and lower meeting rooms were needed places for conferences and families. Both lodges were under construction at the same time. SMR was a growing mountain resort community that evolved each day and every season with more lodge rooms and more cabins.

Getting cabins ready for occupancy was less of a challenge than lodges. There was a difference in preparing for rental the two to three bedrooms compared to getting forty-seven rooms in each lodge ready for occupancy.

Two lodges, Silver Sage and Aspenbrook, a year out. There was plenty of time before opening day, or so was the thinking. Construction crews understand a completion time differently than those who work at the camp reservation and operations level. That mind-set was the potential issue. Construction completion dates could be pushed further into the future, promises of having the lodge ready for guests and guaranteeing that time of arrival that date could not be negotiated. The group would be arriving, and the lodge needed to be prepared.

The time for the group loomed closer and closer, and for some reason, time was speeding up. Each day was another day closer to occupation, and every day it seemed the construction crews were going slower and slower. They were not, but it looked like they were. However, furniture needed to be placed in the building, beds made, curtains hung, towel racks had to be installed and draped with towels, washcloths, and bath mats. If we did not have the rooms ready, we were in violation of a conference contract, but the disappointment of the group was far worse. We had absolutely no choice but to have everything ready when the conference arrived, and rooms, with all the necessary items, were promised.

The day of arrival was upon us, and the forty-seven rooms in the lodge were close but not ready. This was going to be a day of ultra-hustle. Anyone with the breath of life was commandeered to help get the lodge ready for occupancy as there was much to do.

It was decided to start on the lower floor and work upward to the top level. That way when the group arrived, we could begin placing people in the lower level. Silent prayers were offered that the group would show up on time; fervent prayers were dispatched that the buses would show up late, preferably around dinnertime. Practical prayers said we needed to be ready, period.

About midafternoon, the familiar sound of passenger buses was heard coming down the entrance road. The game was on, and the lodge was not quite ready to accommodate the first youthful guests. The first and second floor was just about ready; the third floor was not. Furniture was in the rooms. Linens, towels, bedspreads, lampshades were being installed at a furious pace. The summer staff was a team participating in a coordinated confusion of getting a challenging task completed.

I went to welcome the group leader, but not before changing out of a dirty, sweaty shirt into clean attire and working toward not presenting a stressed, harried look. After greeting the group and suggesting the leaders and I meet with the kids because the need of registering the group had to be completed, stalling for time, the group met in Whispering Pines Chapel for orientation, one of the most complete orientations I ever gave and definitely the longest.

Finally, I suggested we start registering the group, from the first floor to the third. That was the only way to keep working to get the lodge ready. Each name was painstakingly written down, taking a bit more time.

I had a runner telling me the progress of getting the rooms completed. I worked at a snail's pace as the rest of the staff labored at warp speed.

The third floor was pronounced ready. I could see the housekeeping trucks leaving with the crew, and for some reason registration of individuals in the rooms went from snail's pace to full speed.

The youth group was in their rooms. The summer and full-time staff were tired, but the lodge, occupied. At staff dinner that night, there was an in-depth feeling of accomplishment from what had been accomplished that day. Something more significant than the achievements that an individual had been achieved. The greater whole of the meaning of service was completed; it was Team SMR helping others in a humble, yet memorable way.

Did the youth group realize the herculean effort by the staff? Probably not, as the next day as it was back to business as usual for each department. Housekeeping was keeping house, the kitchen crew was cooking, maintenance maintaining, and program offering a plethora of opportunities for guests and conference. This was SMR, a summer of memories, learning, laughing. A loving temporary summer family creating lifelong memories. We grew together that day. We became closer. We were SMR summer staff.

Gary and Coffee Cups

So, I say to you: Ask, and it will be given to you; seek, and you will find; knock, and the door will be opened to you.

—Luke 11:9

Sports of any kind were embraced by the summer staff, softball being the most popular followed by volleyball. Dick Engle and Gary Van Horn are preparing for the coming game. Notice, there was no coffee cup in Gary's hand, which is unusual.

There are things in life that define a person; their mannerisms, habits, likes, dislikes all go into a life blender and whirl around to create just who that person is. Other things describe the event the person is involved in; they may like sports, the arts, perhaps a specific model of vehicle.

Living close together and working closer together creates another set of dynamics. These are the ingredients that when you work with an individual, you get to know them from a personal and a professional viewpoint; you become a team and an extended family. When you are off work, you are still working as you reside on the property. Living on property means you live where you work, which means you live next to the people you work with. You get to know someone in varying levels and degrees more than the standard nine-to-five workday.

Like placing cream and sugar in coffee, the flavor and taste changes. Finding SMR's food service director was easy sometimes; other times, calling in a search party would have been a better plan. Over the years working with Gary Van Horn, I became convinced if Gary didn't want to be found, you might as well not look for him. However, there was one trick that I discovered that worked 90 percent of the time. I used this discovery as well and a few others to find Gary when you needed.

Gary liked coffee. Gary loved coffee. I believe coffee might have run through his veins. Because the kitchen would make five gallons of java at a time, there was an endless supply of this dark caffeinated liquid available to everyone, food service director included.

I discovered that Gary rarely, if at all, ever consumed a full cup of coffee but would leave a partially filled cup in unique and various places around the kitchen, storeroom, dining room, and lodge. The placement of coffee cups was a Van Horn signature that he was at one time there. It was like in World War II, "Kilroy was here," in a sense. All you had to do was discover one little container of joe, and then, if you could, in your search of the elusive food service director, locate another cup, you were on your way to finding the route that Gary had taken.

I would feel the temperature of the first cup, remember that, and locate the second coffee cup; it would be either hotter or colder than the first. Cold, you were going the wrong way; hot, you were hot on the trail.

This game of "find the cup, follow the temperature" was played every day with a high degree of success. One should say that it wasn't that Gary didn't want to be found, not even close. He was always willing to answer questions, solve problems, and look for solutions. That is what a good director of any department would do. He just had this habit of leaving coffee cups around. If some of the coffee chains were around then and he had to pay for the liquid gold, Gary would have been leaving lots of dollars in many places in the lodge and areas surrounding the building.

One would ask, where could you find the trail of evidence starting on the path of locating Gary? The answer is, I would start in the kitchen. Like a hound dog sniffing its way finding someone, I would branch out from the coffeemaker to the next logical spot, his "office." Because Gary didn't have a formal office, I looked for a stack of papers on a dining room table, in the storeroom, or sometimes in an unused conference room. Gary would leave them there, guarded by, you guessed it, a cold coffee cup. From there one would continue to search for the elusive food service director until the success of time, logic, and luck you would find him, only to realize you forgot the real reason you wanted to see him in the first place! Often just knowing you could find him was a victory in itself.

I believe the pressure of crafting meals for people three times a day, seven days a week, month after month is not an easy task, but Gary always made the process look easy. For many years, food was served on heavy aluminum army surplus trays. Later, a change was made to plastic trays, yet the same familiar sections were there. As the nutrition was scooped up and placed on the food tray, you could count on Gary's mantra, "We are here to feed, not to fatten," which then was followed, when Gary was out of earshot, of a brave college student soul stating, "We are here to fast and not to feed." Every summer season each saying would come up, and there was no Twitter or instant messaging in the pioneer years of the seventies to convey the response.

Gary and I lived a few yards from each other in the exact floor plan of modular houses. The only difference was color of carpet and walls. My house was set back from his. Gary worked in the morning. Often I would get home in the early evening, and my vehicle could be heard crunching gravel as I drove past his kitchen porch. I would get out to open my garage door, and lo and behold, Gary was on the porch, coffee cup in hand ready to ask question after question, which needed answers. We would converse for several minutes, and I would try to explain as much as I could with as much accuracy as I could remember. Finally, after a lengthy dialogue, I would drive into the garage, close the door, and be home, only to hear the phone ring. Many times it was Gary with one more question.

Two things happened because of talking with Gary outside to help me be more efficient, or so I believed. One was a fifty-foot telephone cord on the camp phone. Now I could do errands inside and answer questions. The extended phone cord represented the original multitasking in its beginning stages. However, to make the process work, I installed a garage door opener, they were just coming into the home market. I could activate the garage door, get inside, close the door, and wait for the phone call. Now, after looking for the warmest coffee cup from Gary, technology took over; Gary would find me with a simple phone call.

The days of search and find Gary would continue for me. That was inevitable. The process of the "trail of coffee cups" was a proper and efficient process. If I found a cold coffee cup on the railing by the dining room, I knew Gary was now home; he had served another day making meals for the hungry staff and guests.

Soon it would be time for me to go home and wait for the phone to ring.

Hiring Summer Staff

Therefore, everyone who hears these words of mine and puts them into practice is like a wise man who built his house on the rock.
—Matthew 7:24

Early photo of the kitchen staff in 1980. Notice the waitress uniforms, which were required at that time. (Photo courtesy of Kerry Berg, summer employee, 1976 to 1980)

Many sports have a draft to secure the best players for their team. The same is accurate for the hiring of staff for Snow Mountain Ranch and Estes Park Center.

Let's go back to the '50s and '60s when there was only the Estes Park Center. Dad would bring home two heavy-handed briefcases stuffed full of potential college staff who had applied to work at Estes Park for the summer. Colleges generally complete the spring semester around Memorial Day and expect students back around Labor Day.

Across the coffee table, Dad would create three piles of applications. The first collection was by dates. Could the person work from Memorial to Labor Day? The second heap was dated close to the parameters needed. The third pile was questionable if they were summer employable at all, but they were not out of the picture.

In the '50s to the '80s photos, weight, age, and many other factors were answered on employment applications. Times have changed in the current century. Many of these questions cannot be on a form or even asked.

Every Saturday and Sunday Dad would sit in his chair, read the entire application of each person, and place them in one of the three piles. Eventually, a fourth stack was starting to form; these were the individuals who received an invitation for employment. The first stack of applicants began to dwindle in size as the fourth stack increased. As employment positions started to fill, the other applicants eventually found their way to stack number five, not hired. They would not have a summer experience in the Colorado Rockies, at least this year, yet their letter encouraged them to apply the following year, and I feel many did.

After six to eight weeks of weekend culling, the summer staff was hired. When Snow Mountain Ranch was created, the process was similar, but not exactly the same. In the beginning, hiring was decided at the central office, but within a few years, the procedure moved to SMR and the managing director, Dick Engle.

Here is where the process took an interesting turn of events as Dick would share the process with several managers to create the optimum for each department.

Gary, from food service, was the central participant in the hiring process and would express his concerns, desires, and need for a more extensive staff than projected. Glenn was willing to work, teach, and train anyone who was placed in his department. Barb Stemple, in the youth program, wanted a staff dedicated and called to work with children. She would campaign for the best of the best since safety and guidance was a focus for a successful day camp, hiking, and craft program.

Each cabin and lodge room had a phone, which was connected to these two switchboards. Office employees were required to know how to connect and route calls.

Snow Mountain Ranch was a leader in hiring and placing the first woman in the position of hike master. The pioneer spirit was there when Jane Morgan-Bost was asked to take the lead in trailblazing. She said, "It [the hike master position] was the best job I ever had, to be able to guide people on hikes and on my days off to hike. It could not have ever been better. I take a great deal of pride that I was the first woman hike master at SMR. It redefined me and impacted the rest of my life."

As with many staff, Jane stayed in touch with some of the families she had hiked with. Perhaps the continued connection with others is a hidden caveat of the opportunity of being on a staff that will only be together for a moment in time, but that moment lasts a lifetime.

Because of the rapid expansion of facilities and programs, every year was a new "draft" and with new rules for hiring, or so it seemed.

When the ski season was over and spring was around the muddy corner, full-time staff would start to wander into Dick's office looking for the stack of hopeful summer staff that Walt brought from the Denver office on Tuesdays and Thursdays.

Here is where the waiting began. There was a staff meeting over lunch, the ever-present bulging briefcase was present, and we knew it was packed with applications that would be handed over at the appointed time. SMR staff didn't set that time. It was tried once, only once because the look Walt gave to keep your hands off the briefcase was enough to stop the camp director, Dick. He learned a lesson in patience that day.

Every subject under the sun was discussed over lunch. Each moment was in wait to see what the new batch of potential personnel contained in the closed business bag. Finally, like the opening of the envelope at an award ceremony, the briefcase was opened and a fistful of applications, complete with photographs, was handed to Dick. Let the process begin, except for one hitch, the managing director would review them first.

That process of the first review did not deter Gary from interjecting his thoughts as to who needed, desperately needed, to be in food service. After all, each department wanted the best fit for a successful season.

Gary needed dedicated people for the early and afternoon shifts to prepare, serve, and clean the dining rooms. Glenn was looking for persons who could recognize the proper end of a shovel, drive safely, and understand what working outside entailed. Ellen, in housekeeping, needed enough staff to "turn the camp." Check-out was ten in the morning, and check-in started at three o'clock that same afternoon. She needed workers who could work at the speed of light. Barb Stemple was concerned with college students who were willing and dedicated to work with children of all personalities and attitudes. Her staff could not afford to be minus a counselor due to safety concerns. Program staff's agenda changed each day and was altered quickly when the summer afternoon rainstorms graced the camp with their presence.

Of course, there was the office staff, the first line of greeting and problem solving of guests and conference attendees. Business and hospitality thinking was needed as well as the operation of one of the original "plug in to talk" switchboards.

The process of hiring staff was not one of science, of corporate numbered formulas, or any other business guidelines that are in place in today's business models. There was a time of thinking, intuition, and reading what the potential summer staff was wanting and looking for in a summer experience. Working at SMR was not for a significant income or college credit. Many summer staff and eventually winter staff would apply for the experience of a summer in the Colorado Rockies.

"This has been the best summer of my life, nothing will ever be better," stated Kay Gaston as she was saying farewell at summer's end. "No, you will find happiness in so many other areas, your career, marriage, your children. This is one of life's memories of a great summer," I replied. As it turned out, now over three decades into the future, her life was changed by SMR; the memories of a summer working to serve were accented by a meaningful career, with a loving family and a sincere dedication to Christ.

Kay is one of many stories of summer/winter staff that shows the impact of a place where college students can learn, grow, develop a lifetime direction.

It was just a pile of hopeful applications at one point in the process. Little did anyone know a summer of work, friendships, hiking, laughing, and serving could and would change lives. Lives of the staff and the guests.

Looking back on the process, and I don't believe we realized at the time, like all experiences, being a staff member for this brief moment in time was a life-changing, life-redirecting experience.

The process will continue with new parameters not in place in the pioneer years, yet the experience of giving, sharing, and caring will never change. For these are the life building blocks for the future.

MISSING CHILD

*Trust in the L*ORD *with all your heart and lean not on your own understanding; in all your ways submit to him, and he will make your paths straight.*
—Proverbs 3:5–6

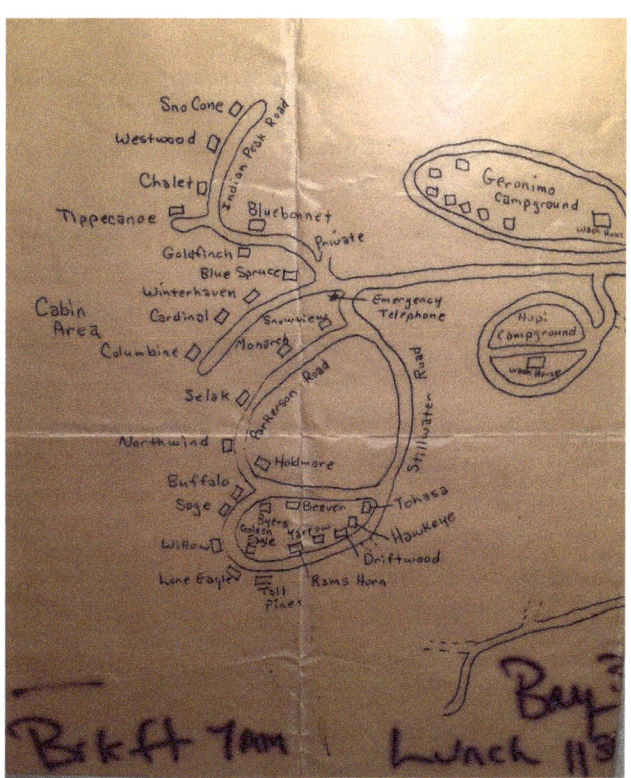

A map of SMR, such as this was used to locate the lost child. Each year, as new construction was completed, new maps would be required to be drawn. Barb Stemple, Program Director, was the designated artist, this is an example of her work in the 1970's (Photo courtesy of Kerry Berg)

The parents forced their way to the front desk, pushing others out of the way. "We can't find our child." Chills and hairs on the back of your neck stand up. With over two thousand acres covered with forests, creeks, streams, this was not a great situation.

"When was the last time you saw your child?" I asked. The reply was he was going to walk to the campground from the main lodge and didn't show up, and that was over an hour ago. It takes under an hour to walk the distance of less than a mile. Doing quick calculations, a child should be able to arrive in half an hour.

Kids love to explore, take an alternative route, and with close to an hour's start, time was critical in two areas, the time missing and it was the middle of the afternoon. Darkness was but several hours away. With night came a drop in the temperature. There was a new moon, so little of any light. We needed to locate this child quickly.

A call was made to the hiking staff and any other staff who could be spared. We assembled in a meeting room below the main lobby of Pinewood Lodge. A map of SMR and topographical maps were spread across several tables. The sheriff's office was for law enforcement support. Grand County didn't have a formal search and rescue team. We would do what we could do. What I knew we would accomplish was finding this family's son, and as soon as possible.

The afternoon summer rainstorm started to announce its impending presence as the Colorado blue sky's changed to storm gray. That was a condition we didn't need as the child was wearing a short-sleeved shirt, shorts, and tennis shoes with nothing else to protect him from the weather.

With each passing moment, both parents were feeling more stressed and wanted to go and look for their son. The staff did what they did best, accommodate and serve by listening and being with the parents.

Groups were assigned quadrants to search, closest to Pinewood Lodge and Hopi campground first. Another search team was quietly dispatched to the cabin construction area as the lure of something being built can be a magnet for children. As circumstance would have it, the construction crew had completed their day, no eyes to see or persons to ask, another challenge.

Food service supplied "comfort food" that few indulged in, yet it was there. In the lost-and-found we located a warm jacket that would work when we discovered the child as it was now raining not so gently.

Every member of the quickly formed search and rescue team would report in over citizen's band radios that didn't work too well, so the teams would come back in after clearing a search area. With each report of not locating the lost child, the parents would emotionally sink to a new low.

A parent will imagine the worst when a child goes missing. Love will do that to you, as you have committed your life to raising, nurturing, teaching, and unconditionally loving this child as they travel to adulthood. When they are lost, you can't do that, and your memory moves down a path of when you last held them, told them you love them. Siblings are even more vulnerable, even though they scratch and fight each other, there is a bonded love that is difficult to break.

We had assigned some youth program staff to the parents and the other children. Their job was to support, listen, and see if any caveat of information could be extracted to bring that information to light. Tears flowed like a loving river from the family, yet the father held the burden of internal responsibility for granting the wish of a child wanting an adventure.

Report after report came in, no contact, no trace. Another excruciating hour went by. The word was out in the campground and among other guests of the critical situation. People interrupted their vacation to offer any and all assistance.

One guest was a counselor and offered his services to the lost child's family and also to the staff as needed. He was welcomed into the search headquarters. A few moms took the missing child's mother and, in the corner, held her and held a prayer for comfort and safety.

Another report called in the news was the same, no sighting. Time and weather continued to be the enemy. It was like the earth was saying, "I dare you to find him." We took the dare; we would succeed.

Eventually, the rain subsided, and the gray clouds gave way to clearer skies. Dusk was not far away; twilight was too close. Darkness was announcing that it would be here soon after sunset. Moods matched the impending night. Hope continued to push back against the open feeling of no control.

Prayers were continued to be offered as more people heard about the situation. Whispering Pines Chapel became a place where whispers grew to fervent prayers. There was a gathering in the chapel to bring to God's altar the safety and location of a family's child.

Another report filed with the same results, no sighting, no rescue. Hope was not lost, but there was a feeling of hopelessness.

The search teams had looked in most of the designated quadrants, dinner had been missed, no one cared. There was only an appetite for finding this family's child; the food didn't matter.

Desperate, scared, concerned, helpless feelings as the forest is a large, daunting place and no place for a child alone as evening started to creep across the landscape. Staff knew the trails, but a child would not. Tears of immense desperation flowed, some visible, others hidden in the souls of the parents and staff. Time and darkness were the worst enemies you could face looking for a lost person. Soon the summer chill would command the falling temperature. Keeping a positive outlook was a challenge, and yet there was always hope.

Prayer upon desperate pleading prayers continued to be said. More guests came, offering prayers support. Hugs were in abundance. No one wanted to see a child alone, lost, cold and in danger of spending a night in a forest. The reality of such a scenario was becoming more and more an actuality.

One of the front desk personnel came into the room and motioned me to talk to them outside. The look on the employee's face was not one you could read. Was this good news, bad news, or was there a decision to be made about a conference as camp operations needed to continue?

"You need to talk to this person," she said. We walked upstairs and to a sight of coming joyous reunion. There, with one of the ranchers, was our lost child. "I found him around one of my barns, he was crying, scared, and lonely." You could see where the child's tears had cleared away the dirt of being lost and probably falling several times. "I thought he might be from here, so I brought him back." What an understatement. All I could say was thanks, and I asked if he wanted to meet the parents, which was turned down because of evening chores.

We walked downstairs to parents who in an instant went from the emotion of sorrow to unbounded joy. Child, parents, siblings ran to each other in a lifetime track race. Hugs, kisses, more hugs, mother inspecting, father relieved, siblings figuring ways to use the incident to their advantage, and lost child safe in the arms of family. He was protected by prayers. A grace of continued mercy covered the family like a comfortable blanket.

We called all teams in, made sure we had a full head count, folded the maps, packed up the room, and returned the area to a conference meeting room. The desperation was over, a family was together, and summer staff was again summer staff. Perhaps bound together in a tighter weave with the tapestry of memory.

Operations returned to normal. The next day would bring another challenge, another adventure, and more memories. But for today, the day was counted as good. I turned off the lights in the meeting room, but going into that place in the future always brought back the memory of God's protecting grace, reuniting a family and taking a concerned situation and God showing His glory. The lost was found, just what Jesus does, which we did somewhat on a human scale.

Cutting Firewood

You see that his faith and his actions were working together, and his faith was made complete by what he did.
—James 2:22

Highly efficient and well built, the tractor and saw were a primary production item to cut the many trees that were cut down for roads, structures and to help the surviving trees to prosper in the harsh winter conditions.

One of the ongoing chores at SMR was cutting firewood, and no one was immune to the task. This was because the land was forest, and roads needed to be established, areas cleared for guest cabins and lodges. The trees were cut down, stripped of their branches, and piled to be transported to an area where the logs could be cut to the proper length for burning in the many fireplaces on the grounds.

This twofold process of getting the logs to the wood cutting pile was in many respects the simple part. Getting the wood ready for fireplaces required more cutting and lots more time. There was a wood-cutting crew hired to do the chore in the summer. They would rotate with other maintenance crews as the task of wood cutting was long and could be tedious and thankless.

Glenn Tilghman had designed a system involving a Ford tractor manufactured around in 1950s. First, the machine needed to be repaired as it did not run well. Glenn, as always, brought back to life broken vehicles, such as buses and tractors that were required to forge a vacation center from a forested homestead.

He designed a belt-drive system that would turn at high speed an angry-looking circular saw blade, which then would slice logs into firewood. Also what was needed was a moving platform to hold the wood during the surgical process of sizing. When the repairs to the tractor were finished or the design of a woodcutting device was complete, a set of exact verbal instructions were sternly given to the college student operators as these machines were not the safest in any sense of the word. With Glen, they learned to follow instructions.

Each evening after the dinner meal, Carl Mayes would make an announcement that he was off to the woodpile, and with a practiced look at the people in the room, he would ask how many would like to go and have the experience of cutting, loading, and hauling wood. As the summer progressed, the enthusiasm of the offer waned. Yet there were still those who saw this woodcutting activity as fun.

Teams were formed, and the challenge of the number of wood hauled, stacked, cut, and stacked again became a bragging point at the next dinnertime. Sometimes the woodpile for burning was over six feet tall. It seemed it was considered incorrect to arrange the wood in cord stacks. Who would want to do that when you could haul, cut, and toss the cut logs? Where what the fun in that?

One evening I listened to Carl's announcement, request, and almost threat about the fun of cutting wood. There had been several days when this activity had not taken place, and few of the staff still had the itch to cut wood. I could see Carl and a few others were going, but I was off to my office to catch up on a few things.

After a while, I was finished, and the evening was prime for a drive around the property. I had forgotten about the woodcutting offer and traveled the road that would lead me past the evening's event. Or so I thought I would drive past. Not planning my evening drive route became a verbal opportunity for Carl to holler at me and invite me to participate in this evening event.

Needless to say, I was upset at the offer. I had a full day and just wanted to drive around the property, find a quiet place to watch the evening capture the day into night. I was not in a mood or a right place emotionally to mess with dead trees. I stopped, parked my car, and slammed the door, which nobody noticed because of the noise of the buzz saw. I don't think you could have even seen the door closed because of the increased number of wood chips and sawdust that was being launched by the whirling blade.

The staff that was there was having a good time, but they were short of a few people. Carl asked if I could help fill one of the trucks that would travel to the Estes Park Center and supply them with firewood. He offered me a pair of gloves, but being a bit in the negative attitude side, I declined, another mistake as newly cut trees have sap. At the end of my stacking process, I could almost pick up a log with the amount of tree juice on my hands and arms.

We worked for about two hours. The truck was filled and ready for delivery; all of us had chips and sawdust in places we didn't want it to be. The chore of woodcutting was over for the evening. Before we left, we sat down and shared the day as the sun created tall shadows across the fields and blanketed the mountains with an evening shadow.

It was a time to reflect on the day, picking wood off our clothes and tossing it at each other. Carl, with his Cheshire cat smile, listened to the vocal evening's chatter. There was a bonding of this wood crew, a bonding that would only last as long as we sat around on the stumps of trees. I believe each of us knew this time was a special, one-of-a-kind time. We would continue to work during the summer as a team, but not this team like we were now. Tired, laughing, sharing, and listening differently to each other.

A campfire was suggested, and the idea was rejected as it could mean we would need to cut more firewood soon again. The fact we were sitting on what could be considered a large pile of wood didn't matter; we would not sacrifice one log to a fire. Besides, with as much sap and timber stuck to us, a single spark could be devastating to clothing.

Carl stood up, signaling it was time to go, thanking each of the crew for a job well done. The wood truck was scheduled to travel the next day, and it was ready for the journey.

I got in my car and was ready to complete my original plan of driving around camp when Carl came up to the car window, which I had left down, and now I would be cleaning wood evidence out of the car. It seemed I had parked downwind, and wood likes to travel sticking to the outside surface and getting inside the vehicle. I didn't need a seat belt. The goo on my clothes could have held me there.

"You want to drive the wood truck to Estes tomorrow? You could leave at early light and be back by noon or so." I imagine I had a look that could freeze water as I did not see this as a need to further my career. Carl smiled and laughed, and then said he knew I didn't want to be cutting wood this evening. He said he didn't either, but the task needed to be done. He thanked me and said he was just kidding about taking the truck to Estes; he would do that. If I were not stuck to my car seat, I might have considered a negative physical response. Woodcutting can build character; it did that evening for me. I would not have changed the evening in any other way. Later, I laid my head on my pillow, reflected on the day, still picking wood out of my hair. This day was a traumatic experience for me that ended very well.

Whispering Pines Chapel

And I tell you that you are Peter, and on this rock, I will build my church, and the gates of Hades will not overcome it.
—Matthew 16:18

Whispering Pines Chapel –. Since 1971, this chapel has hosted worship services, Bible studies, weddings, conference meetings and as importantly quiet times for guests to reflect upon the glory of God. (Photo from author's collection)

When Pinewood Lodge was constructed, there were plans to build a chapel at the same time. The design called for an octagon-shaped structure with a vaulted open beam ceiling. The architecture was unusual for the area, as was the plan of Pinewood Lobby with the high vaulted ceilings and expansive windows. But bold is bold, and Whispering Pines Chapel would prove to be just that.

A large cross was placed prominently at the front, erasing any doubt this eight-sided structure was indeed a Christian place of worship. The board minutes reflect the direct desire of the board that a place of worship be constructed as soon as possible, so it was done.

Whispering Pines Chapel has a history of weddings, meetings, movies, and programs. Rudy and Clarabelle would give their pioneer talks to the guests and staff there, and lectures and group gatherings were scheduled.

Colorado author and teacher Robert Brown presented Colorado history using two slides of a ghost town in their prime and how they looked at this time in history. Sunday services were held. Weddings, funerals, and memorial services were scheduled and offered.

Conferences inspired countless people to direct their lives toward Christ and dedicate purpose to His will.

Colonel James Irwin, who walked on the moon in 1971, selected Snow Mountain Ranch for his High Flight conference. Irwin and his staff helped returning POWs and missing-in-action families at the end of the Vietnam war. The conference participants gathered each day to continue the healing process. PTSD was not named in the mid-seventies, but attempts made to heal the wounds of war were offered, and Whispering Pines Chapel was there for such a purpose.

The camp setting as cloistered as SMR was, could have been a deciding factor for the High Flight conference. For many, the chapel was a place of comfort, worship, even a safe sanctuary for the reunited and waiting families.

At the close of the High Flight conference, I had the opportunity to walk with Colonel Irwin down the road to his lodge room. As we walked, the moon shone from behind a cloud, streaming its light on the way. We paused and looked up at the shining orb high overhead. "Can you believe you walked up there?" I inquired. I was and would forever be earthbound. He sighed, gathered his thoughts, and said, "I cannot prove except by my NASA orders that I was up there. I have no proof except a piece of paper that states I will travel to the moon and back with government meals and housing." He then looked again at the moon, shining the evening-reflective light from the sun, and completed his statement. "Like the Bible, you have to believe my orders, they are my only proof. Jesus came to earth to share with mankind eternal life. That is what is far more important than a trip to the moon and back, far more important."

We walked in silence the rest of the way and parted with a handshake and a thank-you for a great conference. He then said, "Jesus walking on the earth is more important than man walking on the moon." In 1991 Jim Irwin became a resident of heaven, far beyond the moon. The poem that inspired his foundation is found at the end of this chapter. High Flight Foundation continues to help many people in need and be ambassadors of goodwill across the world.

There is a quiet presence within the walls of the chapel, a sense of power greater and higher than mankind. Preachers, instructors, and staff have presented Sunday services in the chapel.

One Sunday in the mid-seventies, the piano accompanist was not able to participate in the church service, which meant the congregation would be singing a cappella. An announcement was made at the beginning of the service to this fact, and an appeal was presented that if someone, anyone would be willing to at least play the proper beginning note for the hymn, it would be a blessing.

A hand went up, and a gentleman who was camping came forward. "I can help," he said and proceeded to humbly ask what was needed besides just a note for the beginning of the hymn. Would it be okay to raise the key at the third or fourth verse of the hymn? Was there time for a brief prelude and a postlude? Would a classical or contemporary style be acceptable or both? What about during the pastoral prayer, perhaps a quiet background could be played? This person, who was never named nor was the denomination given, was the principal pianist/organist for his church and generally had two Sundays off a year to sit with his family. He had just given up half of that family time to give back to the many families attending the Sunday Service.

Yet perhaps for all the activities, the most meaningful service was the annual Cross and Communion Service that was scheduled for the close of the summer.

The chapel seating would be arranged in a setting that gives a feeling of comfort. Many times, the design was in a circle, other times a half circle. Every time, God's loving presence was there. Summer staff sensed this was part of the closing of the summer experience. A farewell dinner had been prepared and served, and now a communion service was offered. Summer was coming to a close. This staff, who had been given orientation at the beginning of the summer, was now being provided another form of direction at the end of the summer in the chapel. Small crosses were given to each person who attended. The service, held by candlelight, a message delivered with intense love, combined with hugs and tears of joy, signaled what was now would never be the same again. The summer was becoming a time of memories, a calling to continue life somewhere else.

The chapel, a gathering place of program and worship, now was giving a final direction to seeking and searching college staff who had gathered from across the country. They had worked, played, hiked, laughed, cried together for a brief moment in time. Cross and Communion in Whispering Pines Chapel was the closing of the summer's experience, yet the opening of the continued life's journey.

Over the years, when staff would come and visit, we would talk and recall the summer they were at SMR. As we walked and shared, we would end up at the door to the chapel. When we entered, there was always a pause with a time of reflection. In the stillness of the confines, you could almost hear the memories of a summer past come rushing back. The gentle wind wandered through the pine trees outside as time traveled to a time of service, a summer now but a memory.

Whispering Pines Chapel will continue to hold programs, worship services, and other events. Perhaps its most significant purpose is to quietly be available for a person, a family to enter and sit and listen to the internal thundering yet whispering voice of God that speaks to your soul.

HIGH FLIGHT

Oh, I have slipped the surly bonds of earth
And danced the skies on laughter-silvered wings;
Sunward I've climbed, and joined the tumbling mirth
Of sun-split clouds -- and done a hundred things
You have not dreamed of -- wheeled and soared and swung
High in the sunlit silence. Hov'ring there,
I've chased the shouting wind along, and flung
My eager craft through footless halls of air.
Up, up the long, delirious, burning blue
I've topped the windswept heights with easy grace
Where never lark, or even eagle flew.
And, while with silent, lifting mind I've trod
The high untrespassed sanctity of space,
Put out my hand and touched the face of God.

—John Gillespie Magee Jr.

Summer Staff Musical, 1981

> *Shout for joy to the LORD, all the earth. Worship the LORD with gladness; come before him with joyful songs. Know that the LORD is, God. It is he who made us, and we are his; we are his people, the sheep of his pasture.*
> —Psalm 100:1–3

Every summer, staff is uniquely different, each center being blessed with a staff that is talented, often in music or just the desire to want to share what gifts they have. The summer of 1981 was such a musical staff, not that in all the other summers I was at SMR there wasn't musical talent—there was. However, the summer staff of 1981 was composed of more than the usual musical talent and had the desire to participate in something far more significant than themselves.

A conference had been booked for a few years called Choral Arts Seminar, which consisted of music teachers from across the nation who taught voice and conducted choirs from high school through college. The seminar was designed for the teachers to have a chance to listen, sing, and purchase new music for their school, college, or university. For a week, Whispering Pines Chapel would be resonant with the sounds of close to three hundred music teachers sight-reading new music. The composers from the music company were present to showcase their arrangements and tunes.

During that conference time, SMR would sound like a music school morning, noon, and night. The death of Richard Rogers, of Rogers and Hammerstein fame, bothered me. These icons of the mighty four musicals as I called them, *Oklahoma, South Pacific, Sound of Music,* and *Carousel,* were bouncing around in my brain starting in May before staff arrived.

As May was a slow month for business, I felt the creative urge to take all five and arrange some of the music in a way to create a tribute to these melody masters of memories. I didn't have a clue what the summer staff would be composed of from musical talent, but I felt a compelling personal direction to create something that would be fun and entertaining for the summer staff to perform.

June arrived, and so did a staff that looked like they might be able to succeed in presenting such a program for the summer guests. Imagine, an evening of Broadway music showcasing a summer staff most of whom are not music majors. Yet they have a passion for singing, memorizing a script, and then creating a magical evening for other staff, guests, and the community.

Rehearsals started mid-June, and a date was set for one performance in early August. The only requirement to perform was the desire to participate. About twenty staff said they would like to be a part of the plan. As the summer progressed, more staff stated they wanted to be a part of this summer musical event. There were opportunities for stagehands, publicity, ushers—the job list grew with each person who volunteered.

It is fascinating creating something that is more than you, yet with something you wrote and directed, you see a weaving of commitment, talent, and maturity. A few rehearsals before opening night, I felt that it was time to tell the Snow Mountain players that this production was owned by them. I had taken my inspiration as far as I could. Now they were in charge, as a troupe, and in control from now on. Together they would and could set the final direction and personal touches to the performance. The tribute to Rogers and Hammerstein was now also a tribute to the staff for their gift of time and talent which would soon be openly shared with other SMR staff and guests.

It was theirs to give away with all the love and talent God had blessed them with. My work was complete.

Opening night was a night of unbridled enjoyment as the staff sang, danced, joked, and shared their hearts for a one-time performance, or so they thought. Remember the Choral Arts Seminar that was going to have their meeting on grounds? The leader arrived early and came to the performance. He liked what he heard and asked if they would present the program the final night of the seminar to all the choral arts teachers and composers. Without thinking, I agreed. I felt the troupe would love to go for a second show. After all, there was almost a full summer of rehearsals, and two concerts are better than one.

In Pinewood Lobby, the afternoon of the next performance, a well-known composer was holding court with teachers and other composers. I always liked listening to this person's sage and thoughtful advice as they continued to freely give their gift so others could excel in their career. At one point this person called me over. "So tonight is the night for your staff's musical revue, right?" I said it was. He replied, "Are you nervous?" My answer was, "Not really, the troupe had this." "Well, I would be very nervous if I were you. Do you realize they will be performing for people who know every word, and line, the nuance of these musicals?" I had not thought about that and decided to keep that thought to myself as I broke out in a cold sweat.

The performance that evening went off with only one minor line being spoken early and then repeated at the right time with resounding laughter from the performers and audience. When the audience was asked to join in with the classic final song "Edelweiss," there was not one person in the room who didn't know the notes, the lyrics, or the harmony. It was a once-in-a-lifetime choir, singing together for the first and last time. A memory seared into the hearts of all who were there. A blessing beyond the emotional horizon, something for each person to carry in their souls forever. A standing ovation went on for about five minutes and gave the staff a boost because soon their summer would end.

Word of the performance was carried over to Estes Park Camp where the dedication of the new auditorium was to take place after the annual membership dinner. The YMCA of the Rockies Board had finished their summer meetings. We were asked to be the first entertainment in the new auditorium. Again the gifts of one staff were presented to the Estes Park staff, the YMCA Board, and all the members who attended the membership dinner.

Sometimes, an idea, the smallest spark of inspiration, turns into a wildfire that builds upon itself. That summer, God crafted a staff willing to serve beyond the usual, to give up their time in the evenings to rehearse, to learn lines and songs. They learned to give back to others and beyond themselves.

The talent and desire were present and used for the memory of a summer staff and to the glory of God. We were blessed with the right people at the exact place they needed to be, at Snow Mountain Ranch as summer staff.

More than just a musical tribute happened that summer, I believe many staff found a life direction, something not expected from a summer job in the Colorado Rockies. Not anticipated but found.

From songs from a musical to a decided direction in life, all this was completed under ninety days. Not too bad for a summer, but the blessing continues each summer. The staff of 1981 grew together, increasing in personal and group strength. Then, years, sometimes decades later, looking back, I believe there was a paradigm shift in thinking that would bring a person to see their life calling. This calling would set a positive life direction and is one of the hidden jewels of Snow Mountain Ranch, Estes Park Center, including Camp Chief Ouray. This opportunity of commitment could be one of the hidden caveats in the substance of the YMCA of the Rockies.

THE CHAPLAIN'S KIT

Jesus looked at him and loved him. "One thing you lack," he said. "Go, sell everything you have and give to the poor, and you will have treasure in heaven. Then come, follow me."
—Mark 10:21

Pictured – the Chaplain's Altar Case carried by military chaplains for many decades. Some, I am told have bullet holes in them, all are worn in many places. Chaplains serve a critical mission for the freedom to the US and allied troops at home and abroad. (Internet photo)

Sometimes you just fall into opportunities, and then you lose that opportunity. Then years later there is a reunion of sorts of something of the occasion or object left, once considered lost and now found and returned.

This is the story of a suitcase that could be made into an altar for military chaplains. It is referred to as a chaplain's kit.

Summers at Snow Mountain Ranch were filled with opportunities to meet families and individuals from all walks of life. Often, you run into a person, and a conversation starts, then one thought leads to another and another. Before long you discover there are many things you have in common. Talks with military and former military gravitate toward time in service.

At some time, you discover each of you has had a common ground in serving your country. In this case, the revelation was that we both had served in the United States Air Force. He was an officer, assigned as a chaplain. I was a photo technician and worked in the public information office. Now, I oversaw the programs at Whispering Pines Chapel

As we talked, he mentioned he had a chaplain's kit and was not using it anymore and wondered if the ranch would like to have it. "We would be honored," was my reply. We could use this for vespers outside the chapel; it would be a perfect focal point. He said when they came back the next year, he would bring it with him. We continued to talk about service in the military, and he told me about his various tours of duty, Stateside, Korea, Vietnam, Europe, and back to the States, taking the chaplain's case with him on all his military tours.

He talked about what was contained in the kit and said all the vestments were there to have not only a service but communion as well. This kit was issued to military chaplains of all branches.

A year passed, and his family was once again guests at SMR. I didn't know if he remembered, but one day he came into my office with a black rectangle box with the initials "US" emblazed in gold by the handle. "Here is what I promised you last year," he stated.

The black worn case was set on my desk. The latches and handle were well used; the case had seen some rough times. The chaplain moved his hand over the case as in a final farewell. I sensed he was saying goodbye and hello to a new ministry for the kit at the same time. We opened the case to a musty smell of storage and many years and miles of travel that had been seen in its service. The aroma was a fragrance I had never experienced; it was as if this scent was reserved for this specific type of case.

As he opened the kit, two sides could be unfolded to increase the size of the altar as the top of the case was designed to stay upright. There was a blue velvet material made to cover the top and the unfolded sides making a makeshift altar stand.

The rest of the storage area held a chalice and a cross that was either a cross or a crucifix depending on which way it faced. Two vials could contain anointing oil, small communion cups, a container for unleavened bread, and a little dish for the bread. Basically, it was the things needed for a church in a box.

He handled each object with loving care of memories that each vestment held for him. I wondered how many times he had set up the kit. How many times in peace and then in a war zone had he hurriedly stowed the items as danger approached. He shared stories of having to carry it personally as the kit was more critical than luggage since his Bible was always stored in the kit.

After some time, we returned the items to their nestled place in the battered, battle-worn kit. We closed the cover, snapped the latches. The kit was ready for travel and another adventure.

I thanked him, promised I would take care of the kit as best as I could. We shook hands. He said he was leaving tomorrow, and I realized the retired chaplain had kept the chaplain's kit with him until a time of departure. The chaplain had held on to it as long as he could. He patted the box. "Thank you for wanting this. I hope and pray you will be able to use it for the Lord's work." One last look and the transfer was complete.

Over the next several years, the chaplain's kit was used in services, both in Whispering Pines Chapel and in religious events around the ranch. Each time I would remember the kindness of a military chaplain that gave a case of manmade objects for eternal work.

Several years later, I left Snow Mountain Ranch and the chaplain's kit behind. There was a debate in my mind as to whether the kit was more a gift to SMR or to me personally. I was always responsible for the equipment when I worked there; now I was moving on.

In the end, I believed it belonged to the ranch. I placed it in a safe closet, hoping it would be of continued service. In many ways, I was entrusting a precious friend into the service of others.

God continues to work in His mysterious ways with His timing. Thirty or more years later a message was sent to me asking me if I would want the kit back as it was discovered under the chapel stage. I had left my name on the equipment, and somehow that embossed sticker had survived over the decades.

Contact was made, and in a fast-food restaurant, the lost kit was returned. Once again, it was placed on a table, the latches were again undone, and the top opened with a protest of hinges not cracked for a long time, only to find an empty box. The cross, chalice, serving dish, communion cups, all gone, disappeared.

Yet the familiar musty smell of the kit was present. Memories rushed back from the first time the kit was opened on my office desk. Sadness enclosed my mind of what used to be there and now was not. Each place where a chalice, a cross, and more were held for safe transportation was empty, empty like a tomb.

I was disappointed by the material loss; however, looking at an empty kit, where there was nothing, I knew there was more than just the return of the hollow case. The smell of mold and travel made me realize that as empty as this was, it still was full. Full of the promise of our Lord returning someday. Unfilled now, yet the lingering fragrance from years past was there as a reminder of a promised return.

We closed the black box, secured the latches. I thanked them for finding me and returning the empty case. Yet the weeks of the excitement of seeing all the vestments in their place was disappointing but for a moment. However, the sadness of an empty case was overpowered by the compassion of a gift returned and the knowledge of knowing nothing is lost when one believes. That was the lesson of an empty chaplain's kit, and it was well with my soul, very well within my soul.

The Doctor and the Mechanic

A Story of Hope and Friendship

But seek first his kingdom and his righteousness, and all these things will be given to you as well.
—Matthew 6:33

This is a story, like a fairy tale, but derived from facts.

I would like to tell you a story about the doctor and the mechanic and the chance meeting they had because each person and their families went on a camping adventure in the Colorado Rockies.

It is said that there are no coincidences in God's world, and I believe that is true. A friend and chaplain once said, "God is in control, and He ain't nervous." That is lousy grammar but great theology.

There was a mechanic from the farmland of America that built his own camper. Now back in the 1970s, campers were just coming into focus, and families were experiencing a new trend of staying in campgrounds for vacations. This vacation concept was not new; camping has been around for as long as mankind has cooked over an open fire. What was now unique was you could take your whole family and the kitchen sink with you.

Dad could drive a big vehicle, Mom could cook on her own stove rain or shine, and the kids could bring more than just a friend—they could travel in style with many of their favorite games and toys. It was a new and enjoyable life.

Camping was taking off in America, Kampgrounds of America was opening more and more campgrounds, and many farmers along the highways and byways of this great nation were developing some acres of pasture for the traveling public.

And so a mechanic and a doctor caught the camping fever. One loaded his family in the converted school bus, complete with bunk beds, kitchen, living area, and a less-than-desirable ride with no air-conditioning. But it was camping, and the family was looking forward to a great time in the Colorado Rockies.

The doctor, on the other hand, purchased a new camper called a motorhome, with all the amenities of home. It had a kitchen, double bed, overhead bed for the kids, TV, radio, cassette player, cruise control, and air-conditioning. After all, when you purchase an RV with the name Winnebago Chief, you would have all the comforts of home.

Each family packed up anything and everything needed for the trip to the mountains of Colorado. Not much was left behind. Even the family pet was loaded into the rolling real estate, and they were both off.

The mechanic arrived before the doctor and was settled in a few days before the doctor, and the doctor's family showed up in their new all-decked-out RV. The mechanic watched as the family unloaded every possible piece of camping equipment and set up what looked like a permanent mountain home, except on wheels.

Life was good, crisp cool Colorado air, warm days, campfires at night, children running around and time to "just lazy," the mechanic was thinking.

As the mechanic watched, he noticed that when the doctor arrived, the big RV was not running so well. The doctor was overheard telling his family he would have to be gone the next day and hopefully back that night after getting repairs completed. He would be away for a day, not in the Rocky Mountains, and not with his family and the activities they had planned.

With all the talking and commotion, this got the mechanic curious as to what was going on. Being inquisitive, he struck up a conversation with the doctor. He asked the doc, "Why are you going back to Denver when you just arrived here?" The doctor replied that his new RV was not running as well as it should and he needed to take it to a dealership for repairs. He also said he didn't have a lot of time to spend with his family because of his profession and the time in the mountains was more than precious to him and losing a day was more than unfortunate.

The mechanic asked what the problem was, and the problem was explained to him as well as could be described by a person who heals people and doesn't understand mechanical things. The doctor also said he was looking forward to the next day's activities as it was a hike he was excited about and the whole family had agreed to hike together. Now, he said, the planned hike would happen, but without him, a real bummer.

The mechanic suggested he take the hike with his family and let him look at the RV. After all, he was a mechanic and knew the workings of a vehicle. Anyway, he could learn something about RVs and perhaps fix the doctor's RV at the same time.

So the doctor agreed and let the mechanic work on his RV. The doctor would take his family on a day hike; the mechanic would plan his day looking at the sick RV.

When the doctor and family returned from the day hike, tired but relaxed, the mechanic was relaxing at this campsite next to the doctor's. The children of the two families joined up to create a combined family mountain adventure, and the two couples sat down. "Well, your RV is fixed and will run fine," stated the mechanic. "It was an easy repair, and I had a chance to learn a lot about RVs and systems."

The doctor replied with thanks and asked about the cost of the repair. The mechanic thought for a moment and stated, "No charge, it was something I chose to do." He just would not take payment for the repair.

The doctor gave the mechanic his business card and said to keep in touch and said thanks over and over again as family memories were made for a lifetime on their family hike. He also said if the mechanic was in Texas sometime, come and visit and if he needed anything, just call.

A few days later both vacations were over, and the families packed up their respective vehicles, the mechanic headed east to the Iowa–Nebraska area and the doctor back to medicine in a large metro area of Texas.

Each person repairing and each diagnosing symptoms in their respective professions and each family remembering the vacation in the Rocky Mountains. Life returned to the way it was, and all was good. Or so the mechanic figured.

He received a call that his father was quite ill and to go immediately to a hospital in Omaha. His father had experienced a massive heart attack. The x-rays confirmed the diagnosis, and the outlook didn't look good. A second opinion was suggested, and that is when the mechanic remembered the doctor.

Overnight delivery for packages was in its infancy. The mechanic called the doctor and asked him if he would look at his father's chart and x-rays to confirm what the trusted medical staff was saying was true. The doctor agreed and looked at the records of the mechanic's father the next day. Then the doctor called the mechanic and stated the diagnosis was indeed correct; his dad needed heart surgery.

After a brief pause, the doctor said his surgical team had been approved to do the surgery in Omaha if the mechanic would agree. "After all," the doc said, "I am a pretty good doctor and an excellent heart surgeon."

So the doctor, his team, and all the needed expertise flew to a farming community from a major Texas metro area to perform a delicate operation on a person they only knew as the mechanic's father. The surgery was successful, and the mechanic's dad would be okay.

After the surgery, the mechanic asked, "What do I owe you?" The doctor replied, "Nothing. You see, I chose to do this."

There were two families, two professions both in the business of repair and restore who met in the Colorado Rockies. They became friends over a campfire and worked to support each other's family with the skills God gave them.

Each a player in God's orchestra, each having a solo part so that the rest of us could listen to His still, quiet, thundering voice as he brought two families together, by His plan and not by coincidence, not by chance, but a divine providence.

That is a small part of resort ministry, a large part of God's world. That is the story of the mechanic and the doctor who found support across a campfire; it would not and could not happen any other way. This was in God's plan.

SUMMER CAMPFIRES

*May the grace of the Lord Jesus Christ, and the love of God,
and the fellowship of the Holy Spirit be with you all.*
—2 Corinthians 13:14

*One of the fun evening activities for me was singing and playing
my guitar for staff and guests. Hearing voices singing in unison,
holding onto a stick roasting marshmallow over an open fire, add
chocolate and graham crackers and this concoction was, just the best.*
(Photo from author's collection)

Sometimes the windows of heaven open; often this happens at a family campfire. Each week SMR program department scheduled at least one gathering around burning logs, either behind Pinewood Lodge or at the Rawley Homestead.

There would be singing, s'mores, a crackling fire, and of course, tall tales were always told. Many on the summer staff had the talent of playing guitar and leading the favorite campfire songs of the time.

Songs by Peter, Paul, and Mary were famous in the '70s as well as many of the leftover folk songs from the '60s, which were generally requested. Sometimes the campfire song leader would have a good idea of where the majority of the families were from based on the songs requested and which ones were asked to sing first.

States such as Iowa, Kansas, and Nebraska leaned to the non-protest songs of the '60s and '70s. Whereas families from Texas always wanted and knew all the words to "The Yellow Rose of Texas." There was an understood rule that college and university fight songs were unfamiliar to the song leader. There was no good reason to get an academic rivalry started at a family event.

Campfires generally started around seven in the evening, as the sun was setting, and the cloaking of an evening sky would be present a few hours later. Logs to sit on were arranged in a circle around a rock-barrier fire pit. Maintenance would have a good supply of wood available to create a comfortable, warm, and inviting fire. The food service department had all the ingredients for the three-item recipe of s'mores, which was graham crackers, a chocolate bar, and marshmallows.

At the beginning of the campfire, there was a feeling of many people and families. With the creating of s'mores and the singing of familiar and new songs were sung, the individual families became a temporary family group, but just for this moment.

What was always amazing to me was the number of families that had no idea what a s'more was or what the term meant. Growing up in a resort setting, s'mores were part of a staple diet. Instructions as to the "how to" would be given, and people charged with the incineration of the marshmallow. Some people liked the charred, burnt sugar item, others were up to the challenge of creating a perfect golden-brown melted-in-the-middle sugar pill. Of course, that took a lengthy amount of time, and some children or adults just could not wait that long. Many a burnt white, now blacked marshmallow was consumed right off the stick it was cooked on.

The crackling of the fire, the strumming of a guitar, and the singing of an impromptu family choir created an atmosphere for a few hours that could not and would not be duplicated ever again on this side of heaven. Even if the same individuals and families came together, the next campfire would be entirely different.

As the sun gave way to an evening sky, a magical transaction happened. Subtly, as the sky darkened and the campfire became the ember of coals, everyone moved closer together, closer to the crackling warmth of the fire. Sparks lifted heavenward, as in many cases the rush of the day; the stress of work seemed to lessen with each crackle of the fire. It was as if the sparks drifting their way upward were taking the concerns and carrying them away, then burning out.

Requested songs were now more introspective; songs about the beauty of life, commitment, cares, and concern were asked to be sung. The campfire song leader always had a few easy songs to be sung and would interject them into the singing at the appropriate time.

Many times, voices in harmony would start to join with the chorus of song as the evening moved on. People became familiar with those around them and felt comfortable venturing along a harmonic path. Sometimes a person would comment on how beautiful a person's voice sounded and would ask if they could sing a song for the group. There was always a pause, the children would urge the person to do just that, and now a concert accented by a crackling campfire, with burning wood for accompaniment, including the guitarist, would ensue.

Often the smoke from the fire would bring people closer together as everyone played musical logs. The wind would drift from one direction to another, and many people would move away from the smoke. It became a known fact that the campfire group would be going back to their lodging all smelling like smoke; that was part of the memory of an evening shared around a fire.

At some point, the music ceased, and conversations would start with the question of, "Where are you from? How many years have you been coming here?" If anyone wanted proof of a world made small by people, all you needed to do was listen to the answers to the question of, "Do you know so and so in your area?" Another joining of a thread of family tapestry in God's continued loving world.

Nightfall would arrive too soon, and the embers of the campfire would start to die down, and someone would toss another log on the fire, the original meaning of "log on." Far different from today's definition with the cloistering of people looking at a tiny screen, many with earbuds jammed into their ears.

As one looked up at the starry sky, the embers of the campfire traveled toward the treetops and beyond. You could almost touch the stars, and somehow you did, sitting there listening to the singing, the sharing, and the spontaneous laughter of a group moment in time.

Soon the event would end, the fire would be out, and the coals of the campfire would be doused cold with water but not before a final, closing song.

The African hymn "Kumbaya" was generally known by everyone, and if you didn't know it, one verse and you were an expert in singing this campfire favorite. "Come by here, my Lord," the translation of the title of the song was precisely what has happened at this and many more family campfires.

Come by here, Lord. You did. Your presence was felt in the warmth of the fire. Your majesty was presented with the beauty of the Colorado Mountains, from the highest peaks to the minuscule flowers along the hiking trails and in the fields. Your eternal music was heard in the wind wandering through the trees and the sound of the forest. From human singing and laughter, Your presence was in the forefront of families brought together by the event of a campfire where many became one family for a bright moment in time.

You came by, stayed a while, visited, yet you left a memory of singing, s'mores, stories, and just perhaps friendships that will last beyond one campfire in the Colorado Rockies.

The fire now has died out, the singing concluded, a guitar was stored once again in its case, and the evening was brought to a close. Over, but never forgotten because memories are like pioneers who welcomed weary travelers to their campfire. Those who were here were given a gift that is written in their hearts.

Fall Solstice

FALL COLORS

*Your eyes will see the king in his beauty and
view a land that stretches afar.*

—Isaiah 33:17

This painting, by Martha Wiggers, has hung in our house since the early 1970's. Martha and her husband would vacation at SMR, she would paint, and staff and guests would stand in line to purchase her work. The path shown here I have walked more times than I could count. (Photo from author's collection)

Toward the end of August, morning frost becomes the introduction to fall in the Colorado Rockies. The air has a crisp sharpness that one can feel, signaling a change in season. The days continue to be warm, but the warning is there. Fall is coming, and soon after, winter.

Fall is a precious time of the year as the green leaves of the aspen trees start to change from the high country to the valleys below. The change is gradual but decisive. One day the brilliant green of the aspen leaves begin to show a dark green color as the trees prepare for a winter's slumber, only to be reborn again in the spring.

The wind takes on a firmer intensity, somehow knowing its role will be at the forefront of fall and winter storms. Where the sun was primary for the summer, wind and lower temperatures take the life cycle stage of seasons now.

Summer groups have departed, the flurry of activity of June, July, and August are replaced by the impending snow. But first, the pallet of fall beauty must and will happen. Each day you witness a gradual change as God casts the announcement of fall in the changing colors of the aspen trees.

The transformation starts at the highest altitude trees and descends its way down the mountain to the valley below. The green of the leaves gives way to the yellowing color of fall. Followed by a rainbow of orange and red to add accent to the yellowing colors. It is as if God took the three fall colors, dipped paintbrushes with those colors, and splattered them, through design, upon the mountains and the valleys.

In the summer the aspen leaves create a sound from the breeze not easily described but remembered with comfort, and in the fall the sound of the wind through the leaves brings a particular announcement of the departure of warm and longer days to the impending knowledge of a lowering of temperature and shortening of daylight.

Fall in the Colorado Rockies brings forth a litany of vehicles filled with folks all wanting to view the explosion of color. People, families, and gawkers from the city become day travelers journeying to the mountains for the viewing of the coming slumber of the aspen trees. This is a characteristic time, I suppose, with these road trekkers.

If one ventures past the steering wheel and passenger windows of the automobiles and decides to walk a trail into the woods and journey through the aspen groves, they find peace in the roaming. The stillness of the bright, crisp air, mixed with the fall breeze and the rustling sound of the aspens buffeting in the wind, brings absolute completeness to one's soul.

One day I started walking at SMR. There were many trails to take, and I chose one less selected, but with the knowledge I would be in the royalty of the aspen groves. The ground had a firmness about it because of the continual lowering of the temperature. The morning held a frost that would give way as the sun battled a losing summer temperature battle. I walked in silence listening to the rhythm of the earth, hearing the screech of an eagle accented by the crunching of ground under my feet and feeling the expanse of God's creation from the smallest fallen leaf to the bulk and girth of the mountains that surrounded and protected the valley.

Each step was a traveler's opportunity to look deeper, with the sunlight cascading through the leaves and creating a dance of shadows on the ground. Above, the trademark Colorado blue sky stood as a sentinel to the reality of the presence of God. No evolutionary theory could have painted this piece of eye and ear candy that I was witnessing and being a part of.

Chipmunks were storing their final loot for the long winter's months. Flocks of birds were flight mapping their travels to the south. I thought of the anticipation of skiers, cross-country trekkers, and snowshoe enthusiasts watching the fall sky and knowing the winter's snow statement was not too far behind. It was only a matter of time before simple hiking would be in memory.

The quiet rhapsody of fall created a feeling within a person that you were one of few in this area, and the privilege of that knowledge allowed you a deeper appreciation of the experience of hiking in this season.

Looking up through the aspen grove, you could see an artist's palette of colors. I stared perhaps for only a few minutes, but to me, a lifetime observing the gentle, yet striking beauty of fall that was expressed in the simple transformation of color was a gift to be remembered.

Finally, rounding a bend in the trail, I could look across the valley, and it was at that moment, I began to understand the intimate vastness of God. From where I stood I could see the panoramic creation of the Continental Divide. The mountains as watchmen of earth, pointing to the sky and heaven. The accented scattering of colors of the visual pronouncement of fall to the valley below soon to be covered with snow for the winter's months.

The fall hay crop had been harvested and stored for winter feeding; fences were again secured for the safety of winter livestock. Many homes and lodges had their supply of wood for the chill of winter.

The earth was getting ready for winter, but for now, this moment, fall had not released its authority of the season. I turned to start my travel back home, but took one last look, one last moment to place in my memory and to picture in future years.

I was blessed to be here at this moment in time. Blessed to have the opportunity to claim this part of the earth as my personal territory, even if it was just for a moment. Blessed with work surrounded by the beauty of living in the Colorado Rockies. This moment was a holy time; I was in the sanctuary of God.

In silent prayer, I spoke a gratifying thanks to God for His wisdom in the creation of planet Earth and His love of myself. If humans were made in His image and this planet was created in six days, we have the responsibility to share His love, grace, and mercy to all that we know and would be meeting.

My walk back was a purpose far more significant than just to look, observe, and appreciate the beauty of what I saw. I was finding a meaning of direction in life to serve His kingdom and glorify Him with all my actions.

I prayed I could do that. I knew I would, because my days were invested in God walking beside me, even on a fall day, through the aspen groves of Snow Mountain Ranch.

Weather and Alone Time

I lift up my eyes to the mountains—where does my help come from?
—Psalm 212:1

The Colorado Rockies creates interesting weather patterns. From the mountain-drenching rains in the summer to massive snowstorms in the winter months, with snow sometimes so deep it will come up to the roof of a small mountain cabin.

In the spring, a new awakening begins to a world that was almost entirely once white, and now splotches of earth colors reappear for the first time since late fall.

Leaves on aspen trees start to regenerate from the slumber of winter; buds protected now venture forth as each day increases with extended sunlight and the warmth of spring that will turn into summer.

Fall will give way to winter, then the other seasons will take their turn during the sequence of seasons. That is the continuing cycle of living in the high country of Colorado. One day sunny, another day there will be snow or rain, but not for the entire day. Weather changes in Colorado constantly. There is a saying in the Mile High State, "If you don't like the weather, wait five minutes, it will change."

Each season brings a time to reflect. A time to wander the myriad trails that you did not have time in the busy season. To become lost in a God thought process. In the fall, especially, I would meander off to gather my strength of emotion from the hills. During the spring thaw, just sitting in the warmth of the sun was enough to still my frantic emotional heart.

During the busy summer season, many people would seek to have the same experience, to hike among the majesty of the Colorado Rockies, to embrace the outdoors and all that nature offers. To find a moment of solace and comfort in the process of foot travel. These hiking traveling times were never enough. How can one have enough of what God has created?

The challenges of working, serving families, and groups was always an opportunity for giving to one or many. That was my job, to help ensure a quality and value vacation time for families and groups. I was a resident of the mountains. They were a limited guest for only a week or two, perhaps just a few days. Therefore, the needs and desires of the partial time they had requested were a priority to the staff and to me.

In the early years of Snow Mountain Ranch, the fall season was a time of low, if any reservations. Many times, there would be several weekends where no guests were on the property. It would be you and the wind promising winter soon would arrive. This was a time to catch up on projects placed on hold, maintenance not addressed, and to take some much-needed downtime.

You would shift your work schedule to accommodate personal and social activities that had been neglected during the summer months, and it was also a time of errands upon errands in Denver that were not possible in the summer months. This process would be repeated in the spring after the Winter Park ski area closed.

For now, it was a quiet time in the Rockies. This precious time was a time I cherished as I was able to ground myself in what the guests saw and felt by being on the property.

In the busy months of summer and winter, the coordination of all aspects of running a resort was a priority, and one tended to get caught up in the administrative and corporate firefighting of resort work. You would lose sight of what was the paramount reason families and groups chose to vacation and conference at Snow Mountain Ranch.

Driving, walking around the property in the slow time between the seasons was a way to reconnect to see what others saw in coming here. You could get a refocused sense for the beauty of the area and the blessing of the camp setting. Knowing and remembering the unique and special place SMR is was essential to me.

With the changing of the aspen leaves in the fall, the statement the wind and the temperature were making, I could feel and embrace what SMR meant to others, but more so to me. Deadlines could be pushed back for even a few days; it was vacation time in a sense. Sitting on a lodge porch, lounging in many of the lobbies of the lodges, it was a time just to soak in, like a dry sponge, the living water of where you worked.

You had the time and the comfort of that time allowed you to not only appreciate the buildings but a higher calling of hiking the many trails, listening to nature. Listening to yourself, but more importantly, taking a moment, some time, quiet time to pay attention to what God wanted to say to you. You could almost hear that soft, thundering voice talking to you, giving you strength in direction. Showing you His grace in the rustling of aspen leaves, or the sound of a gentle wind upon your face accented by the warmth of the sun.

This was a time cherished. Soon winter would be here; the schedules of meals, check-in, check-out, and buses to and from the ski areas would be the focus. But for now, at this moment, all the ranch acres, every trail, each couch or chair was yours alone to appreciate and slumber with your personal emotions. The din and dun of people were absent, an eerie feeling to say the least. Generally, the lodges and public areas were packed with the human tide of people talking, laughing, and anticipating their next high-altitude adventure

I believe we all need time alone, and I firmly believe we require this alone time with our Lord. When we are silent and we push the Pause button on the schedule of events, we will hear His voice, but only if we listen and are willing to listen. There is no confusion in God's direction; there is a whole lot of muddling around when we don't pay attention to what He has to say to us. This prized time of silence is like fuel for your drained emotional and physical tank. By taking in the quiet, pausing, you become recharged, filled and ready to do what is needed to be completed and to serve who are necessary to be helped.

But for now, the wind, the sound of that wind through the trees, the ever-changing clouds in the sky, this was your personal sanctuary, your own universe of which you shared with God, and that was good, very good.

First Snow

*I call on you, my God, for you will answer me;
turn your ear to me and hear my prayer.*

—Psalm 17:16

Tabernash General Store – The small town of Tabernash, for many years housed most of its commerce in a tiny store. This photo says a lot. As you see, it has the bus station sign, an outside phone booth, a Pepsi product sign, and a motorcycle that is parked in the snow, along with a gas pump and even a mailbox! Inside the store were supplies and other needed products. (Photo, Greg Albright, author's collection)

Each fall, you know winter will be arriving. Every year, you, with many others, wait until that first snowstorm arrives and signals fall is over, and the marathon for the winter is here. It is time to be snow-shovel-ready and winter-ready.

I would generally take vacation time in late September or early October, arriving back home just before the end of the month. It seemed to me, the first winter snowstorm, the one that would blanket the ground always seemed to arrive just in time for Halloween. More often than not, I was right.

The days were crisp with winter temperatures, the evenings just cold, and many mornings the snow generator of the weather pattern had completed its task of dumping more snow. For the ski and snowmobile business, this was what they were waiting for.

We would receive calls inquiring about how much snow was on the ground from families and groups. Sometimes the reservations for these individuals were several months out, but they wanted to know about the snow depth and what the winter was shaping up to be.

Snow Mountain Ranch was changing from the spattering of fall colors to the continual white of winter accented by the green of the pine forest. Yet some days, when the snowfall was particularly gentle and the wind absent, the bows of the pine trees were laden with snow. The tree's adornment was like white snow feathers, and the bending branches held that visual glory until the wind caused the fall of the white feathers.

Every day was a different view, yet each day was the same, white crystals covering the ground in more depth with the snow. Winter had arrived and with it the opening of new opportunities for maintenance and the program department.

The first snow is welcome because it signaled that valuable downslope experience that many people moved or visited the mountains for, skiing.

For me, the first snow was the opportunity of seasonal change. From outdoor activities, now to more time indoors working with families and groups. I would watch the white flakes accumulate, covering the ground, knowing the chill of the weather and the warmth of being inside was a blessing and comfort. Hearing the crackling of a good fire in the main lodge, all the ambiance of the blessed high country living that was all year for me but only a few days or weeks for so many others. How can someone not be thankful for living a blessing such as this?

With each intricately designed flake of snow, the landscape of Grand County was being transformed into a wonderland of white blanketed beauty. Winter was becoming a resident for the next six to seven months. The moisture created by the snow would eventually give way to the lush goddess of spring, then summer.

Winter, for me, was an investment for the summer months. An asset of moisture that gave great emotional and visual returns to one's soul that could be seen in summer flora. I welcomed the snow, appreciated the chill of the morning and the warmth of the sun that would generally follow. You didn't even consider washing your vehicle until late spring. Grand County brown mud was mixed with what was the color of your car. There was not a reason to clean; within in a mile you were back where you were before washing. Besides, it was a badge of honor to have a car that was dirty. That helped make you a resident of the county.

Every morning, Monday through Friday, I would drive my daughter, Jennifer, to the entrance of Snow Mountain Ranch so she could catch the school bus to Fraser. The school bus was generally on time, but the few minutes we would sit and wait, the vehicle heater blasting warm air keeping us warm and the windows from fogging up, we would have a precious few minutes to talk.

One particular morning it was a time of reflection of identity for Jennifer. She was feeling lonely, out of sorts, in some ways abandoned by a person she loved. I had sensed her mood the night before and knew she was grappling with these feelings. So this day, we left a little earlier. I was also hoping for the school bus to be just a few minutes later than usual.

We talked about her feelings, her eyes reflecting what she felt and an occasional tear trickling down her face. Such a young grade-schooler to be feeling the internal sorrow she was experiencing.

When a child hurts, so does the parent, and I could understand her feelings. We talked about the situation, the definition of what love and family is and how we both fit into those descriptions. Yet I sensed there was more to say on my part, but what?

A quick prayer to God for wisdom and guidance was offered in a silent need. The chill of the morning was gone, the vehicle now warm, and the sun came out showing the expanse of a snow-covered field, glistening with crystals of snow reflecting the sunlight. It was as if there were reflectors on each snowflake, refracting the sun's light back to us. (Or was it the Son's light?)

"Jen, take a look at the meadow. What do you see?" I asked. "Snow," was the answer. "Look again, look closer. What do you really see out there?" Jennifer gazed at the meadow; the rolling drifts of snow and geography started to catch her attention. "I still see snow, but lots more of it."

"Let me tell you what I see, I see thousands of reflections of light glistening from the snow crystals. What I see past this is God showing you how much He loves and cares for you but sending His love to you in the glistening of the snow."

Jen looked some more, and from sadness, a joy was formed in its place. She saw and understood the beauty of one snowflake after another because this was a display of God's love. Her face now showed happiness.

The bus pulled up, and she was out the door. She turned around and said, "I love you," and was off for an adventure in learning. A moment captured in each of our hearts because of the reflection of something as miniature as a snowflake, but as grand as the universe.

Perhaps that is the reason I like the first snow of the year because as the depth of the snow continues to build, I can see God's love building and melting the heart of a child, one reflection at a time.

WINTER ACTIVITIES

Opening Day of Ski Season

Anyone who runs ahead and does not continue in the teaching of Christ does not have God; whoever continues in the teaching has both the Father and the Son.

—2 John 1:9

After a summer of endless activity and a fall of corporate regrouping, cleaning, and maintenance, the opening of ski season was always looked forward to. There are a few bragging rights in the Mile High State as to which ski area opens first and closes last. Winter Park has not been an early opener or closer, but they have always been a ski area of quality. Somehow the snow is better at Winter Park and Mary Jane was known as the Jane, all you have to do is ask the locals. They will let you know how proud they are to ski the mountains of Winter Park.

Snow amounts start to be mentally measured before the snow begins to fall as enthusiastic skiers and workers start making predictions as to the quality of the season, the depth of the base and when the lifts will open. Every year, it is the same conversation, to the extreme skier, it is the only conversation at this time of year.

Throughout the summer months, snow-grooming equipment has been repaired, maintained, and readied for the season, as well as the ski patrol's snowmobiles and rescue equipment. Ski rental shops have increased their inventory. Disposed of worn-out skis. Many people take the broken or used skis. You will see summer fences being constructed from such equipment.

The ski area never completely shuts down as lifts that convey the masses to the top of the mountain need to be maintained, safety checked and rechecked. Crews are mindful of the need not only for reliability, security, and protection but also for speed as no one wants to be stranded on a ski lift or a lift that is slow.

What the winter months have destroyed, the maintenance of buildings and equipment has repaired. It is a busy time to be ready for the opening day of ski season. If you are a fan of any sport, you know the anticipation of opening day; it is the same with ski areas with snowballs thrown in for good measure.

Skiers become cloud watchers, looking for the coming of the next snowstorm. If that storm is strong enough, it might mean a day-earlier opening. They become amateur short- and long-range weather forecasters, with one prediction in mind, snowfall. Although that opening date is set, it does not mean a personal tour of the ski slope could not be in order. If there is a full moon, a willing snowmobile driver, and a few daring skiers, game on.

A ride up the slopes on the back of a snowmobile and a glide through untracked snow under a full moon is too tempting for the addicted skier. Then the bragging rights come in. You were first, you skied before others, and the next morning, if it does not snow that night, your tracks will be evidence someone was there. Several laws of mankind and a few of physics were more than likely broken, but you skied first.

For the recreational skier, opening day involves several personal physical activities. The summer has been kind to you, but not to those legs and muscle structure for skiing. Many exercises will help you feel the burn as you strengthen those legs.

Walls become your friend as you do vertical push-ups whenever you are standing in line. Stairs, two or three at a time up and down helps. Hiking in the summer months is excellent, but it does not involve skis on one's feet and muscle tone changes.

With each snowflake that falls, every day is another day closer to the opening of ski season. It is a matter of time now. With snow accumulating and increasing anticipation of the sensation of gravity sending you down a white slope, the winter's cold, and a season ski pass, you are ready. Ready for the snow fun to begin.

PLOWING SNOW

We ought, therefore, to show hospitality to such people so that we may work together for the truth.

—3 John 1:8

Snow can be your friend or foe, it all depends on how you look at it. It is in what way you address the challenges of the chore of moving snow off the roads, shoveling from sidewalks, and sometimes scrapping the "white champagne" off the roof of cabins and lodges. At the close of the ski season and with spring coming, plowing, shoveling, and scrapping snow, you begin to believe that any more snow to remove is a nuisance that need not be tolerated. Enough snow is enough.

There were many days when it would start snowing and not stop for a day or two. This weather pattern required constant removal of the ski product. The ski areas were elated with the new snow, but vehicles laden with excited skiers needed to get to the slopes. After all, ski groups and families came to ski. Getting a vehicle unstuck from the clutches of the ever-increasing amounts of snow dropping from the sky was an unplanned activity of a ski vacation that needed to be avoided.

Snow Mountain Ranch (aptly named) had the necessary removal resources to keep roads clear, but that also meant staff needed to be working with the equipment to keep the streets open and the sidewalks clear.

Families checking into their cabin were advised not to park too close to their cabins as the metal roof was designed for the snow to slide off. However, the driver, wanting to get as close for unloading luggage and supplies, generally is not familiar with what would happen when a mini roof avalanche would occur. The soft thumping of snow cascading to the ground was the first indication your vehicle was now a snow drift, held tightly by the compacted snow that fell from the roof. What you had walked through a few minutes before, you now had the opportunity to walk upon.

A call would be made to the front desk explaining the dilemma because somewhere under a pile of snow was a vehicle needing to be released before the spring thaw. A crew, usually, two winter employees, would be sent to the cabin with snow shovels in hand to start the digging-out process. This assignment could take a long time depending on the intensity of falling of the snow.

In many incidences, another call had to be made to maintenance from the snow removal crew on site. The project required machinery that would release the vehicle from the grip of winter's frozen folly. Glenn would travel the over-mile distance to the cabin site of the issue, using a small tractor to shove back snow on the roadway as he made his way to the site.

On arrival, a discussion would take place about just where the car was, with Glenn generally saying, "Heck, I thought I was here to just plow the snow back. Nobody said anything about a car being buried."

Here is where the expert talent of one person would come into play. A John Deere tractor can demolish and crush an automobile by its weight and traction alone. Playing hide-and-seek becomes a delicate game not to be taken frivolously. Glenn would scrape the fallen solid white concrete away from the car. This event became an impromptu program for not only the family but for a few cabins in the area as well. This happened just after they moved their cars further away from the cabin, lest they become the next opportunity for their car covered in a snow casket.

Inch by inch, with the owner watching and with help from the staff, the car would emerge from the mound of snow, now to be moved to a safer area, and that part of the work was done. Glenn then would proceed to push piles of snow away from the house, forming a parking area that could accommodate several vehicles. It was Glenn's way of keeping ahead of the storm and creating a pleasant parking experience for the guests. After all, how many people have observed the skill of a heavy machine operator delicately giving freedom to a snowbound car?

Cabin snow removal was one of many tasks that needed to be addressed. However, the removal of masses of snow on the roads leading from the cabins and lodges to the entrance was another matter. There are many miles of roads that require constant maintenance of removing snow, and this is not an easy task to accomplish.

Many times, the roads needed to be plowed more than once, depending on the amount of snowfall. With one way in and out, a stuck vehicle efficiently closed the camp to any travel.

Glenn and one other person would sometimes have to start plowing and pushing snow back in the early hours of the morning to have the road passable for ski traffic. When the temperature was twenty below zero, and the wind was whipping around, it was a cold, dangerous, and unpleasant night to be outside. You were exposed to the harsh elements as there was not a heated cab for the equipment. One person would plow, and the other would push the snow back further off the road, so when more snow fell, there was a place to shove out of the way. If this were not done, Snow Mountain's entrance road would become a less-than-one-lane road.

One time, a ski bus going too fast for conditions skidded and came to a halt, blocking both lanes of traffic. I could see there was a problem when cars were backed up and not moving. If they were stopped at Pinewood Lodge, where I was, I needed to know where the problem was. I got in my four-wheel drive vehicle and skirted around the stationary cars. That was a challenge, but seeing a bus sideways on the road was a shock. On the other side of the bus was a car, not a foot away. The passengers were inside the vehicle, wide-eyed and thankful no contact was made.

The question became, how do you get a bus turned ninety degrees and facing down the road back on its way to the ski slopes? You call Glenn to bring a tractor to drag the bus around, getting it to be in the right direction. This procedure takes time, and skiers have little time to waste, as skiing is paramount. Those first runs are always the best in a skier's mind.

The challenge of the situation required time and space to drag a forty-five-foot mechanical whale around on the road without damaging road and bus. There was a tow hook on the front of the ski bus, which required Glenn to drive the little but mighty tractor over the snow piles hooked on to the front and to pull the bus back into the road. With that task completed, the backed-up traffic wanted to get past the bus, out and to the ski area as well as did the passengers on the bus. We had the makings of a winter NASCAR race.

When the bus was on its way, traffic started to move in both directions, and the issue of the road being closed was resolved. I got back into my vehicle, passing a constant stream of cars. Looking in my mirror, I could see Glenn shoving snow into the trees, making the road even more passable.

It was morning, and the day was just starting, and Glenn and the snow plow crew had already been up all night. This would be another long day with little sleep, yet with a whole lot of commitment to serving others. There must be a golden snow shovel for snow removal crews in heaven. I would imagine Glenn would have several shovels for the tireless, frigid, dangerous nights he was willing to keep the roads open.

Group Arrivals: Nighttime

And the lookout shouted, "Day after day, my lord, I stand on the watchtower; every night I stay at my post."
—Isaiah 21:8

Whoever said that everything has a place and order didn't work with youth groups arriving at a ski destination! Many factors tend to go into a group arriving at what would be considered a decent hour. Groups show up when they want to; there is nothing logical about the process. Day, night, after midnight, when the bus pulls into the parking lot, that is the time you get to check in the weary travelers.

Most groups set a time of arrival around midafternoon so that rooms can be assigned, dinner eaten, and meetings started. However, there are circumstances along the travel route. Buses break down, roads become snow packed, and traffic snarls the traveler, to name a few. When you are working with groups, you have seen a thing or two and heard a thing or two.

Staff often was not on duty in the late hours of the evening. That required someone to be on call when the office was closed. After all, having a group arrive and not be assigned rooms was never an option. Some groups would call if there were a delay in arrival, others just figured you were clairvoyant enough to know they would show up late.

Either way, lodging assignments needed to be made, meal tickets distributed, and rules at least called attention to in some fashion. I don't know how many regulations sunk in when you have been domiciled in a sitting position for some time up to twenty-four hours. Nevertheless, procedures needed to be addressed.

I would try to anticipate the possible arrival of groups. A person of prophecy I was not and continually proved that each time I thought I had a handle on when groups would be at camp. Predicting the arrival of a busload of people is akin to herding cats on catnip, not even close to possible.

Some nights, I would see a need to stay up later than usual just knowing the arrival of the elusive group was but a few minutes away. Minutes would cascade into hours, and finally, I would decide to get some sleep, which was the perfect guarantee that a group was pulling into the parking lot. I believe there was an alarm in my bedtime pillow that would activate the arrival of guests. It seemed as soon as I would drift off to sleep, the phone would ring, the dog would bark, my daughter would wake up, and the group was wanting to check in.

Going to the main lodge was a half-mile distance, not much by any standard, except for the fact groups many times were late because of poor road conditions made possible by substantial snow or blizzard conditions. Many times, I would travel on my snowmobile. I knew Gary, the food service director, went to bed early and was up before dawn. I also realized the snowmobile was not the quietest machine in the universe. Sound travels with a higher volume in cold weather. Starting the snowmobile, with a limited muffler, made for a powerful, noisy combination.

I would pull on the starting cord, the mechanical horse would roar to life with enough noise to wake up a sleeping bear, and I was off to meet, greet, and check in a late group. Just for fun and the fact I had practiced a considerable amount, I would come roaring into Pinewood's parking lot at a higher speed than I should have been traveling. Slamming on the brake, turning the skis, the snowmobile would go into a side skid and stop where I parked it. During that skid, I would kill the engine, hop off like some demented snow cowboy, and greet the youth leader, "Hi, glad you made it. Now let's get your kids into their rooms."

The stunned look on the leader's face was worth the show, as far as I was concerned. We would proceed to list what lodge, the room they stayed in, and they were off to high-altitude dreamland. I was on my way back home, waiting for the next group to arrive, and would start the process over again, and again, then again.

Some groups, in their travels, had emergencies which delayed their arrival by one night and into the next day. There was no policy about adjusting their lodging and meal bill, but listening to what happened, we did what we could. After all, in the long run, we wanted them to come back next winter, hopefully, winter after winter.

The opportunity to create policy at the moment was a blessing. You were on the front lines; you needed to make strong, direct, and confident decisions about a situation. Positive reactions and service were critical. Imagine being on a bus with forty high school students over twenty-four hours having an emergency along the way and then being greeted by a staff that was not supportive or friendly. SMR staff bent over backward to defuse the stress and create an atmosphere that was positive for everyone.

Some of the trip challenges were a child lost or a grandparent dying during traveling to SMR. The group needed to get that person to an airport to fly home. Common was a person who became sick and needed necessary medical or hospital attention. The bus company may have underestimated travel time, perhaps directed a longer route. Buses break down, it happens, and as a group, everyone is involved in the process.

Every group check-in—early, on time, or late—was different. Each one offered its personal set of challenges. Groups would state in advance the number they were bringing; that was an estimate. Seldom did a youth group arrive with the number of people they said.

"We had a lot of interest, so we bought a few more," one group leader said. Asking what a few more means, the reply was, "Well, there were so many that wanted to come and ski here, we have two busloads, not one." The question was, "Did you call to confirm there was room?" The answer, somewhat sheepish, was, "I believe my secretary from the church did call." The phone lines must have been down, I thought.

There is one thing about Christian love—it surpasses everything, and with a whole lot of understanding, a problem of such could be solved. Some solutions were simple. The camp had extra rooms. Oftentimes the answer was locating less filled rooms from other groups, making an instant deal to open up lodge rooms and several times combining groups to handle the overflow. Creativity was the corner post of invention. The group was at SMR, and a solution was going to happen. They would have a memorable ski experience, period.

The next day I was asked, did all the groups make it in? Food service, housekeeping, and maintenance needed to know. "Where did you put them all?" The answer was simple and direct. "Don't ask," I would state. It had been a late night, today was another day, and there was another group checking in. That was now the focus.

Group Departures: Not Happening

*Commit to the Lord whatever you do,
and he will establish your plans.*
—Proverbs 16:3

Sometimes the best plans change in a way you did not expect or want. In the high country, especially in the winter, weather often dictates events. Winter snowstorms turn into blizzards, and summer rains become torrential downpours. Add to that the human factor, and plans change.

Berthoud Pass climbs over the Continental Divide to a height of 11,306 feet above sea level. In any season, this pass, because of the road grade, is a challenge for cars and even more so for buses. Engines work more efficiently at lower altitudes. The weather, the elevation above sea level, avalanches, and any other unknown factor can create a change of plans.

In the winter, groups would check out early morning and then ski for most of the day and start a sleeping journey back to their home. Many times, food service would have their evening meal in a bag for the ride home.

When snow falls on a mountain pass, things can happen; unexpected becomes a reality to deal with as the road can be closed for hours to clear an avalanche. At this point, the people who are on either side of the divide are stuck until the road is reopened. I don't know why, but road closures happened at a higher percentage close to the end of the skiing day, trapping a departing group.

Communication was limited to a phone landline. Many times the group boarded the bus and started the journey home, only to be turned around with nowhere to go. The leader would find a pay phone, call, and state their situation. Because SMR was generally full in the winter, the rooms the group had occupied were rented to an arriving group.

Two factors came into play. If each ski group was on the west side of the road closure, there was a more significant challenge. If the arriving group was scheduled for a later arrival, they were not going to make it to the lodge that day. That meant the rooms previously occupied were open for the stranded group at the ski area.

Several times both groups were on the ski side of the closure, and there lies the challenge. How do we place twice as many people in half the space? Here is where understanding, cooperation, coordination, and a little bit of luck come into play.

Each time this incident happened, it was uncharted territory. What worked in a past situation would probably not work this time. Ethically and legally the contract for the current group was primary and would be honored. The departing group still had needs that would be addressed, and in many ways, the situation constituted an emergency. The expense of housing and meals were not budgeted, but the issue had been and would be met and solved.

Housekeeping would be called, and questions about bedding were asked and answered. The only problem was, where could a group of over forty sleep? In one particular case, the only option was to stack the chairs and open the floor in Whispering Pines Chapel for the evening. Chairs were stacked down the middle of the chapel as a barrier for privacy. I often wondered if some or one of the group leaders felt it necessary to rest or try to sleep on the chair stack as a sentinel guard for the group.

Food service would be notified. They needed to plan for another forty for breakfast.

There was a spirit of cooperation and understanding between the departments. The impromptu meeting of the housekeeping, food service, and maintenance departments was brief, and a plan was formulated to accommodate the situation. Each manager would take on the responsibility needed to make the circumstances as comfortable as possible. The group leader was told of the option for not sleeping on the bus and going nowhere to the offer of a "camping out" in the chapel for the evening. This proposal accepted with a feeling of relief and a heartfelt thank-you.

What continued to be the underlying theme every time a challenge such as this came up was a feeling and understanding of the SMR staff of "whatever it takes." We created a positive and memorable experience for guests, and groups.

There were many challenges to surmount, but the teamwork of full-time and part-time staff was continually present. Extra hours were needed to get done what was required. The call was made and a problem solved. Working the extra hour was walking the extra mile and is talked about in the Bible.

This was more than just a job in the mountains, more about the focus of service than doing your described job. It was not a job but a mission, a calling for however brief a moment in time.

Always the question would come up from the group leader about the extra cost of housing and meals. This was a delicate negotiation as church groups had scrapped together only the necessary funds through car washes, cookie sales, and contributions to come on a ski trip. Emergency funds were not thought of or available for situations such as this.

The fact was sleeping in a chapel is not necessarily the usual accepted form of youth lodging, and there was the issue of forty or more extra meals for hungry teenagers. How to address all the expense for SMR and the youth group required solving. No specific policy was ever written to cover situations such as was the case.

Food service department would have the most significant financial impact, and part of the decision needed input from the food service manager. "Look, we always have food left over, let's call it even and give them the meal," Gary Van Horn and then Ron Snyder would state many times in this situation. Housekeeping weighed in. "Bedding is bedding, we can handle the cleaning, we are good here," Ellen Hay offered. "I don't see where anything messes stuff up for us, one more bus is just one more bus to plow around," Glenn Tilghman added.

"Then it is settled, we keep the group as our guests, no charge," Dick concluded. Done.

The process was complete; we were Team SMR. Our focus was to serve, and that we did.

Sometime in the night, the road was opened, only to close again for a smaller avalanche. But by the time the bedding was gathered, the chairs reset, and breakfast was consumed, all lanes of travel were opened, and the journey home could begin for the second time.

Youth being youth suggested another day of skiing. That was not happening, but the effort was recognized. "Thank you for all you did, we won't forget," stated the youth leader. They didn't forget, for the many continued years they came, they would remember the time when people came together in understanding and cooperation to meet a need, fulfill a challenge, and defuse a potential situation.

The commitment of the staff was there. "Whatever it takes" now had a newer and more profound meaning. Profound because serving is personal, a personal commitment to excellence, the definition of SMR staff.

A Silent Journey

Be still, and know that I am God.

—Psalm 46:10

It was my first time out on cross-county skis. There was a full moon, and yet the sky was full of stars. The sky was deep blue with color. Our guide and self-appointed instructor give a few pointers on technique, and we were off. The only sound you could hear was your long thin skis upon the snow. You felt as if time halted, yet in the quiet review you saw, in fact, that you were silently moving.

You would look up and see the sky and then around and see snow glistening from the moon, and you become one with the universe. Unlike any other mode of transportation, we supplied our own. Our muscles worked to get us where we were going. We went as fast or as slow as we wanted. Some call this cross-country skiing or Nordic skiing. But to me, it was myself and nature becoming one, each of us exploring each other as if for the first time and discovering we were a lot alike.

As we traveled further up our route, we broke out of the snow-laden trees and into the meadow. The view was spectacular as we looked at the mountains standing moon-bound like silent sentinels of trees and rock pointing to the darkened sky.

We pressed on toward our goal, an old logger's cabin and a warm fire. Our guide purposely started following us so the novice skiers could sprint out and see how much energy we could expel. Kick, glide, kick, glide. We traveled further, each person separated by the crisp, cold air and their own feeling of self-exhilaration and exhaustion. I was in my own independent thoughts, never knowing how fast or far we had traveled, but just going, moving as suspended by time, or with time as one.

One of the other skiers, out for the first time, remarked as though the universe was all yours, and you were the person who made it go. Or was it that the world which made us go?

I thought about the cities in the valley and all that the scurrying their inhabitants were doing, cursing the snow for slowing them down and working against the clock so they could get back and see their favorite evening television program and be safely locked in their dwelling. Yet here we were out in the open mountain space looking at something, being with someone in a world that we had never experienced in this way, being a part of nature.

We paused. The cabin was in sight. The kerosene lamps inside were lit, and a warm glow was sent out by the uncurtained windows. We could smell the smoke of the potbelly stove and the brewing of the hot spiced cider on the fire.

Our guide and the other skiers went directly inside. I remained outside for a few more precious moments, not wanting to break away, just looking again at the tall pines, the mountains, and the moon.

As I looked up, a jet passed overhead, breaking the stillness of the night. Perhaps the passengers were looking down as I was looking up. I waved, knowing they would never see me, but maybe they would someday realize the feeling of a oneness I now had.

One more look, and then inside, now to remember this night, to always remember.

Rescue and the National Guard

Commit your way to the LORD; trust in him.
—Psalm 37:5

The flashing emergency lights were the first indication that there was a problem. Seeing three sets of emergency lights was even more visual evidence of something terribly wrong. Dinner off property had been a pleasant respite to the challenges of managing the many ski groups and meeting the needs of the guests. Now the lights of an ambulance and sheriff's cars were definitely getting my attention.

While I was out to dinner, the highway had turned into a skating rink. Even four-wheel drives, like I had, were challenged to not slide off into a ditch or a snowbank.

I entered the main lodge, and one of the youth groups was gathering in clusters and praying. The silence of constant prayer was present, and the quiet atmosphere was deafening in many ways. This lobby at Pinewood was always full of noise, of laughter, but not now. The group's leader was in conversation with the driver of the ambulance, and the discussion was laced with a verbal and expressive tension.

The two gave silent permission to join the conversation. "We have a serious problem," stated the group leader. "One of our kids is in critical condition and needs to be transported to Denver for emergency surgery." Recalling the condition of the roads, that statement was an attention getter. "We cannot get over the pass," the ambulance driver said. "The road is too slick and dangerous." That was stated in a voice that relayed the trip would not be made.

I asked if there were any other medical personnel on the property besides the emergency medical crew. I was told there was a medical doctor with the youth group who knew the patient and was with her in the infirmary. It was conveyed that they were afraid this situation might happen before the ski trip, and now a life-threating condition was unfolding.

During dinner, I had noticed an ambulance traveling the route to Denver and a few minutes later retracing its path. I thought that odd at the time, and now the realization was in our lap.

Talking to the doctor only confirmed the criticalness of the condition. The person needed medical help that could not be performed in the mountains, and if not addressed, time would run out for this individual. Their whole life was ahead of them, but not at this moment. All that was in question, and that question could and might be answered in a tragic and final way.

"I don't know if we have a lot of options," stated the doctor. "We simply need to get her to a hospital that has the right staff, the needed equipment, and surgical procedure to save her life." Right now, the world had seemed to have stopped spinning. In several hours another world would end forever.

If there was ever a time for intersession and prayer, this definitely was the time. Word travels at lightning speed in a camp setting. Many other group leaders had heard about the issue and asked what was going on and why the emergency vehicles were here and what they could do to help. This evening of fun started to turn into an evening of prayer as groups were informed of the condition of the individual. What was generally a noisy roller rink now was a silent place of intense prayer as people learned about the circumstances of a member of another group. Still, there was not a way to transport her. Ground transportation was ruled out, and that created only one option. She would have to be flown out, but who could accomplish this, and from where could you get a craft to do the rescue? There was an air ambulance service out of Denver. A request was made, only to be told the weather precluded them from making the trip. It was a dead end, and the word *dead* was not to be recognized. Finally, it was decided to make a call to Ft. Carson in Colorado Springs, where a National Guard medic unit could make the night rescue in marginal weather and back to Denver. It was a shot, a long shot. The call was placed to the army base and was transferred here, transferred there and somewhere else until the person with the right authority could make a decision. They said they would call back shortly.

The weather was starting to deteriorate, the temperature was inching below zero, and the child's condition was getting worse. Time, critical time was running out. The opportunity for a rescue was coming to an end. The phone rang with the statement that an emergency flight was approved, and a medical helicopter was now on its way. There was one requirement: the flight crew would only land at the local airport because of safety concerns of not knowing the area and the darkness.

It was agreed the ambulance could travel the few miles to the airport. The sheriff's cars were placed back into patrol, and now the wait started. A pilot who had a plane at the airport was contacted and asked if he had a radio that could communicate with the helicopter. He said he would do what was needed. There was a public phone at the airport that could be used to summon the ambulance. There was no need moving the girl until the rescue craft was close.

Minutes appeared to turn into hours, and the weather continued to menace the operation with each snowflake and drop in temperature. Prayer continued. Youth leaders, when not praying, were emotionally wringing their hands. In the darkened night, a group of National Guard servicemen was risking their lives for a person they didn't know, and they were on their way. Time, more time was spent waiting, yet God was watching and in charge.

Finally, the pilot's radio cracked the silence with the message stating the helicopter was over the divide and would be at the airport soon. The ambulance was called and sent to the airport, arriving only a few minutes before the landing of the helicopter. The whirling of the blades created a small blizzard, and this was an okay blizzard, I thought.

The transfer from vehicle to airship was completed in a few minutes. The child and the group's doctor were off with the distant *thump, thump* of the spinning blades of the saving aircraft. The chill of the minus temperature seemed warm now, and the evening settled back into a less chaotic routine. Almost frozen handshakes were offered. Everyone departed to a warmer and more comfortable place.

It was over, at least for us. The evening would continue for the ones on the rescue flight. The next day it was learned the emergency surgery was successful; the potential of the finality of life was diverted.

The ski groups realized the authority of prayer, the power of praying for someone you don't know. This was a situation you could have had a difficult time relating to but was answered by the commonality of Christianity. People know each other by the bond they have in the belief they carry. This spiritual, out of His word pledged from a God who has fearfully and wonderfully made people in His own image, spans past any crisis, and many times a disaster is avoided. Yet the glory, as the many groups on their ski vacation realized, goes to God. A lesson was learned on a freezing night perhaps written upon their hearts about the power of prayer and the love of a caring God. Not too bad for a church ski vacation.

Flanagan's Ski Shop

This service that you perform is not only supplying the needs of the Lord's people but is also overflowing in many expressions of thanks to God.
—2 Corinthians 9:12

Outside of brochure, this brochure, along with ski signup sheets, and other literature were mailed to ski groups coming to SMR, allowing the efficient process of rental of equipment. The same pattern is still used in the ski shop today.

"Where can we rent skis?" became a question for the ski groups that would book lodging. There were not a lot of options at the time except at the ski area or renting far away from where you are planning on skiing. The advantage of renting at the ski area was the opportunity for adjustment and exchange, which was the case most of the time.

When you are at a place that promotes skiing, you need to have the support facilities, staff, and rentals that are required to give guests an efficient, positive experience.

It was only natural that the discussion of getting ski rentals on SMR property would come up after many concerns and complaints by groups that they wasted a lot of ski time securing equipment, getting ski bindings adjusted, getting the proper length of skis and the right size of ski boots.

Dick Engle was asked the question, who could supply ski service on site and would be willing to start a business to do the pioneering work? The name of Maury and Glenda Flanagan was suggested. Maury was a ski instructor at Winter Park, and the beginner's hill was named after Glenda, his wife, Mount Glenda. As teaching beginners became more frequent and busier, the second hill was given the title of Mount Maury. At the end of the ski season, there was an event, once titled the Glenda Splash, where local skiers came barreling down the slope in hopes of clearing a temporary pond of water. I suspect each year the water feature was extended a little farther as the entertainment was seeing baptism by self in full ski regalia.

The Flanagans were approached and agreed to give the ski rental venue a try the next season. As with any new frontier, there were challenges. The first was where to place the shop and have ski equipment so groups could access the rentals easily. "We were placed in the bottom of the roller rink, with no windows," stated Glenda. "Because of no windows, many days we took our desk outside and sat in the sun to do our office work."

Once, when the ski group was arriving late, Maury was left in the office to wait for the group, and the ski rental staff went upstairs to the roller rink to have a private skating party. When the group arrived, the Flanagan crew outfitted the group with their roller stakes on!

A building for ski rentals was needed, and there was also a need for a permanent location for youth program offices and a place to go for youth program when the weather was not being friendly for outside activities.

A plan in the spring of 1976 was formulated to build a two-story building. The downstairs for would-be ski rental in the winter and the upstairs for youth activities year around. The following year, Flanagans' Ski Shop was home in a facility that would prove to be a decade-after-decade-long success story of cooperation between two entities working together. Two business establishments trusting each other to do what was needed so groups and guests could have a positive experience.

During the summer, construction was started and completed on the ski shop and program building. The parking lot was designed to be oversized for the buses that would arrive and discharge their ski passengers. The efficiency of the building design allowed potential skiers to enter one door, fill out paperwork, get fitted for boots and skis, bindings adjusted, and ski poles distributed, and exit another door and go back to the bus. Because being young, the youth group would try to ski before getting to their respective lodges.

"We would invent a new way to do something all the time," Glenda stated. "Sometimes we just had to laugh at what we thought would work."

Every fall, the Flanagans went out on promotional trips to talk about Snow Mountain Ranch, Winter Park, and nearby ski areas. Maury and Glenda became ambassadors for not only SMR but the ski areas and their business. "We were willing to do anything, well almost anything, to help the Y."

Many times, groups would arrive at unusual hours. The Flanagans would stay open to fit the group to equipment, even past midnight, and then be back at seven in the morning to open for fitting and equipment rental appointments. "That is just what we did,"

Glenda reminisced. "We did what we needed to do to get the job completed, even if it meant not sleeping."

Lift and lesson tickets were also sold at Flanagans' Ski Shop. There were a bond and trust with Winter Park Ski School and the ski area that was developed over many years of the Flanagans being a vital part of the local industry. "We would have the packet of the lesson, lift tickets, and name tags ready for the leader," Glenda remembered. "That way, when the group arrived at the ski area, all they had to do was go to their lesson, there was no waiting."

One group leader, or perhaps many, would state that getting the overenergized youth group organized was made more accessible because of the efficiency of the Flanagans. The caring the Flanagan family had for everyone was evident for those coming into contact with a family who believed in purpose and dedication to others.

There is something to be said for people who look to serve others, the spark of commitment and direction. Perseverance becomes an emotional firestorm within one's soul. The striving for excellence in the small and large things of life creates clarity of purpose that touches each life.

When the skis were rented, the shop was quiet, and you could almost hear yourself think. Some of the staff would gather their belongings and head to Winter Park. Not to ski, but to be available to adjust a binding, exchange a set of skis, give advice, and many times take returned equipment back to the shop.

Why Flanagan's ?

- Shop located only a few yards from Snow Mountain Ranch Administration Building.
- Shop open until 9 P.M. every night during peak season allowing you to be fitted at your leisure during the evening so you'll be ready to head for the slopes early next morning.
- If you pick up your equipment after 3 p.m., you will not be charged for that day.
- Shop open early enough in the morning to get you outfitted and to the slopes in plenty of time for ski school.
- We sell discounted lift and lesson tickets for Winter Park and SilverCreek ski areas so you need not waste precious skiing time standing in line at the ski area.
- On-slope equipment exchanges available at Winter Park and SilverCreek ski areas.
- Equipment may be returned to our van at Winter Park Ski Area on your last day of skiing providing prior arrangements have been made at our shop.
- Rental equipment may be charged to your Snow Mountain Ranch lodging statement.
- Ski racks which fit most vehicles.
- Ski accessories.

Rental Rates Per Day

	1 day	2-4 days	5 or more days
Skis	$5.00	$4.50	$4.00
Boots ☆	4.00*	3.50*	3.00*
Poles	1.50	1.00	.75
Adult Sets ☆	9.00*	8.00*	7.00*
Childrens Sets	7.00	6.00	5.00

Per Person Rates/Per Day for groups of 20 or more**

	1 day	2-4 days	5 or more days
Skis	$4.50	$4.00	$3.50
Boots	3.50*	3.00*	2.50*
Poles	1.00	.75	.50
Adult Sets	8.00*	7.00*	6.00*
Childrens Sets	6.00	5.00	4.00

*Add $2.00 per day for Saloman boots.
**No Group Rates 12/25 - 1/1

- No extra charge for equipment exchanges
- Breakage insurance included in rental rates
- Rates effective Nov. 15, 1986 and subject to change without notice

Use form on other side for reservations and mail to:
Flanagan's Ski Rental
P.O. Box 302
Granby, Colorado 80446
(303) 887-3767

Ski rental rates from Glenda and Maury Flanagan's Ski Shop. Rates for skis, boots, and poles today are just a little higher.

The Flanagans served groups at Snow Mountain Ranch for several decades. Renting skis was their business. But helping groups, treating them as a family member, was their goal.

The ski shop has been sold; the Flanagans have retired. Maury passed away in July of 2016, yet the legacy of his life will live on. Not because of the shop, not because of excellence in equipment, but because of the human factor of caring and the willingness to travel the extra mile to take a path not often considered, or never considered, by many.

The Flanagans and the YMCA risked an uncertain financial future for a specific focus on being on the front edge of invention. Like the professional athlete who goes for the gold and rushes to the finish line, starting a business is risky at any time of life. Creating a family resort from scratch is a challenge. Summer or winter staff coming from places far away to an unknown destination is daunting. Yet the spirit of exploring, seeking a new opportunity or an untrodden path, becomes not only a challenge for each but, perhaps, a calling to push away from the usual and embrace the unusual. Flanagans' Ski Shop embodies a successful challenge for success. Theirs was a commitment to service.

"We just had fun," Glenda recalled. She now lives in Denver with a view of the mountains from her high-rise dwelling. As she gazes at the Colorado Rockies, her wistful look says it all—it was the right thing to do.

Blizzard Driving

Since you are my rock and my fortress, for the sake of your name lead and guide me.
—Psalm 31:3

Sometimes things just happen. One night, I was home, comfortable and cozy, watching the snow accumulate and knowing this storm would be a grand blizzard. This was one of the worst blizzards I had ever seen since moving to the high country. The police scanner wasn't chattering much as the officers on duty were restricted in their movement of two-wheel-drive vehicles mixed with whiteout conditions. They would go out, but only when called. This was not a night to be out in the elements.

Being warm, safe, and comfortable at home, I was planning an evening to watch TV, but the snow was fighting the signal—snow outside and snow on the TV screen. Finally, the storm won, and I decided to read and listen to music.

Then my phone rang. "Hey, Bob, can you do me a favor?" The call was from Sylvia, Dick's wife. There was a concern in her voice. "I just got a call from our youngest daughter, and she wanted to be picked up and brought home." As the conversation continued, it was clear—even if the weather was not—that she needed to be at home.

Sylvia had told her a few minutes ago, there was "no way we are getting back out" due to the blizzard conditions and the accumulation of snow on the roads. Even the plows were not able to keep up with the white downpour. That was why Sylvia called. Mom's do that, find a solution to a child's concern.

This blizzard was a storm of storms, windy, heavy and fast-falling snow, and whiteout conditions. Everything you need to stay inside and wax your snow shovel. Because when the storm subsides, you will have a winter wonderland chore to do.

"Is there any way you know that she could be picked up and brought home?" asked Sylvia. I replied that if Sylvia went with me to watch the road and direct me, we would get her daughter, Patrice, home. After all, I had a four-wheel drive go-anywhere Ford Bronco, and that should be all we needed. That and a whole lot of prayer.

Sylvia had been at work during the day and knew the roads were getting treacherous on her travel home. I was seeing the full fury of the storm as I started out the door of my house and saw how much snow had accumulated in the brief time I was home. I was thankful that all the SMR ski groups were accounted for. The camp was in a snowball war of massive proportions with the ski groups being the snow soldiers of fortune. They were battling with unlimited ammunition. This snowstorm was a bonus of the ski trip, as there was an endless supply of ammo for an opportune snowball fight. If I didn't know any better, I felt Texas was squared off against Oklahoma, with Kansas and Nebraska weighing in for ally support on either side.

Sylvia hopped in the Bronco, and we were off to bring Patrice home from a lodge in a hamlet called Hideaway Park. Today it is called Winter Park. The snow was just angry and mean. Making our way to the highway gave us a preview of what to expect, and that was everything that defines a blizzard and more.

You had the feeling you were in a giant snow globe that was continually being shaken. Many times, there was a question as to where the road was and was not. There was not an option to leave the road, as that would have caused us to be sheltered in the Bronco for the evening or until the storm quit. This particular menace of snow and wind looked like it was not stopping anytime soon.

We traveled at a snail's pace. The journey that would have taken us less than thirty minutes on dry roads more than doubled in time as we crawled along, many times not knowing where we were, except somewhere on the way. Sylvia's daughter, Patrice, recalled that the snow had a hypnotic effect. The white demon flakes swirled around the headlights of the Bronco as we moved, crawled forward, unsure of exactly where we were, hoping we stayed on the road.

Between two of the towns, we had to travel through a sizeable open meadow. The road, US 40, was straight there, but the wind had a way to make you think you needed to turn one way or the other. Several times, we discovered we were traveling on the wrong side of the road, but the best part was, we stayed on the asphalt. We were the only vehicle that was venturing out, so the highway was ours, not that we really wanted it, but we needed it to do what was requested.

Finally, as the streetlights of Hideaway Park came into view, each of us took a breath. It seemed like our first breath since departing on this quest to bring a person to the safety of their home. Instructions were given to me by Sylvia as to where to turn. This portion of the trip was going to be a challenge as the road twisted, curved, twisted again, and decisions needed to be made as to which turn to make, or we could become lost. The blizzard continued to take its toll on us as we fought back to push forward to arrive at the lodge where Patrice was staying.

This was a time before cell phones and global positioning systems. We were at the mercy of memory, and the thought of "I don't know, this looks right to me as far as I can tell" to locate the lodge in a dark world of snow and headlights. After numerous turns, we located the lodge, with a narrow, steep, driveway that had not been driven on since the snow storm started. So close, yet far away. "What do you want to do?" asked Sylvia. "I could walk up and get Patrice."

"Let's drive up, and turn around," I suggested. There was no need to risk walking the distance. Deep snow has a way of draining all the energy and warmth from you. As it turned out, one out of two options was what we ended up doing. There was no place to turn around. We would have to back down the steep driveway now turned into a cliffhanging experience and call it good.

Patrice was out the door in an instant, in the vehicle, and ready to be home several hours ago. It would be another hour before that would be accomplished.

Backing down a snow-filled driveway in daylight is one thing, but at night, with no references to work from, it was only complicated by the less-than-bright backup lights of the Bronco. Looking forward to backing up was not part of the equation but seemed to help, with Sylvia navigating the passenger side of the vehicle and me watching out of the driver's rearview mirror and looking forward as another reference of where the driveway could be.

Once back on the road, we continued onward, again at a speed where one could almost walk faster sometimes. Down and around the same curves, sometimes sliding on the pavement. But we were moving closer and closer to home. That was the goal and the plan—home. Safely in the comfort of home.

The trip back was like the journey there, snow and more snow. I would stop and clean off the windshield. It didn't matter where I stopped; we were again alone on the road. Other people were either home or sheltered in place at a restaurant or a friend's house.

Back again, across the vast pasture, though Tabernash, a small community that would have been an excellent place to stop, but the challenge of completing a safe journey and the fact we were within a few miles caused us to press on.

Seeing the entrance sign to Snow Mountain Ranch was an emotional welcome sight. If anything happened now, like getting stuck or the vehicle having mechanical issues, we could walk the mile in, maybe. We were almost home.

Finally, we saw the turn to their home. The porch light left on by Sylvia was a beacon of welcome light. In so many ways seeing the warmth of the lights in the windows, it was a comfortable feeling. We had challenged a massive blizzard, found where we needed to go, and returned safely.

I don't credit my driving or the engineering of the Bronco as the deciding factor for success. There were several prayers continued to be offered up before, during, and after this weathered journey.

"Ask, and you shall receive," states the Holy Bible (John 16:24). In any journey, every circumstance, God is beside you. He is protecting you, guiding you, and keeping you safe. When you think back at all the possibilities that could and, in some cases, should have gone wrong, it was His hand of mercy and grace that kept us safe. His love and protection enveloped us in the blizzard.

The next day was a perfect day of brilliant sun and an azure blue sky. The sun was reflecting off the depths of the snow, and each sparkle reminded you of the love of Christ that He has for you. Come to think of it, in that blizzard, the headlights reflected those same crystal reflections in snow as well. That night we merely didn't see the loving beauty, but it was there. There with God's love for us and a mother's love for her daughter. Complete.

A Winter's Sleigh Ride

One thing I ask from the LORD, this only do I seek: that I may dwell in the house of the LORD all the days of my life, to gaze on the beauty of the LORD and to seek him in his temple.
—Psalm 27:4

Winter Sleigh rides are a favorite way for groups, and families to enjoy Colorado snow country.

Winter weather at Snow Mountain can be both beautiful and brutal. The chill of the temperature, crunch of the snow underfoot, and the opportunity to experience God's beauty are all wrapped into each day. Because Snow Mountain was carved out of a Colorado homestead, many of the activities at SMR naturally fell into a style of being on a homestead or ranch.

One activity was the opportunity to go on a sleigh ride on an original hay sleigh, converted to feeding the memories and souls of people instead of livestock. It was always an anticipated event, hearing the jingle of the bells of the sleigh as the conveyance approached the main lodge. It was a new experience, for many visitors, seeing the two-horse sleigh as it glided into the parking lot. I heard and felt the footfall of the giant Clydesdale horses. The bonus for the evening was this night, there was a full moon that reflected off the crystal snowflakes. The weather was a picture-perfect winter scene. Having just had a new snowfall to enhance the picture helped set a festive evening mood.

One needs to appreciate the past to understand the present and to plan for the future. I don't know if going on a sleigh ride would necessarily fit into the current state of family dynamics, but in this particular case, I believe it does quite well.

Even before the sleigh arrived, there was a family that was having a difficult time convincing their young teenage son that the sleigh event would be an enjoyable family activity. He was not even close to the mood to want to sit on hay, be cold, sing songs, drink hot chocolate around a bonfire, and call it a fun family activity. He was very vocal about his feeling as were his parents. He was going to go on the hayride, end of the parental discussion, but not the end of child-angered statement or disagreement.

With such a positive potential for a memorable sleigh ride and the negative potential of a stressed family, I felt that I needed to come up with an alternative plan to help everybody to have fond memories of the evening.

In approaching the family, a plan was starting to formulate in my mind. I needed to get everyone settled and on the hayride and then take a snowmobile to the campfire site and get the campfire lit and burning. My suggestion was to make the young family rebel a helper and take him on the snowmobile with me, thus getting him diverted from the angst he was feeling. Perhaps, just perhaps, we could make a memorable evening for everyone, including the rebel child.

The parents and rebel son agreed to the plan. The sleigh was loaded with cold yet excited families looking forward to the winter adventure. Snow once again started to fall, and I wondered how that was possible with a full moon night and clear skies, but I am one not to question the ambience of God when He creates a life memory moment. As the sleigh slid out of the parking lot past the motorized vehicles, leaving mechanical technology behind, you could hear the starting strains of song and laughter.

Rebel child was not as sure as he was a few moments before, but he was now committed to his personal mechanical adventure on a horse of a different kind. "Hop on, hold on, get ready," was my directive, and we were off taking a different, faster route, for we had work to do.

We bounced along the winding snowmobile trail, dodging trees, branches, and snow drifts and the challenge of not getting stuck in snow over four to five feet deep. The command of hopping on, holding on, and getting ready was starting to make sense to the rebel child as I could feel his grip getting tighter at each turn and bump into the journey.

We finally arrived—survived, according to my somewhat disgruntled passenger—at the designated campfire pit. As I turned off the machine, the quiet deafness of a mountain wilderness replaced the noise of the engine. You could hear and see your breath. The moon was the sentinel in the sky, a white orb of light casting eerie shadows from the trees and drifts of snow. Quiet was the night with the crystals of moonlight reflecting off the snow. We stood for a few minutes listening to the earth breath in silence. A coyote somewhere in the distant let out a mournful howl that got the attention of the rebel child, a person of city life. He decided to stay a bit closer to the only human he knew was on earth!

We gathered up the wood to create a combination of a campfire and bonfire. It was instruction time for the city child. Because of the cold and the sound of wild animals, he was a fast learner. With a *whoosh*, the fire was lit, the wonders of a fire accelerant, or Boy Scout juice as I liked to call it. We both watched as log after log succumbed to the flames and the heat of the fire pushed back against the cold. The crackling of the wood, the sparks snaking their way to heaven, and the occasional howling of a coyote was the music of the evening.

The silence of the soul became the conductor. I looked over at the rebel child. Part of the rebel was gone; he was watching the fire, turning himself occasionally to keep each side of himself warm. The evening was having an effect on him.

We talked about his school, family, and friends. Subjects came and went as fast as the coals of the fire continued to ignite. The glowing embers of the campfire created the reunion for the first time of two former strangers listening and sharing thoughts. These moments of thin spaces that God creates in His universe are, I am convinced, life-mark changes. We may not realize it at the time, but in time we see clearly what was cloudy at that moment.

Another few logs on the fire and the former rebel child was now the campfire master. My work was given over to this young man, and that was just fine with me.

Suddenly, you could hear the sleigh bells signaling the impending arrival of the sleigh. Then, faintly in the distance, you listened to the laughter of caroling as the snow sled came closer to its destination. "Listen, look, what you see you will perhaps never view again," I stated. The rebel child looked at the sound as with each breath and stomping of the horse's hoofs. The sounds became louder and closer, now accented by the campfire, starting to welcome the chilly travelers.

The moon cast its evening light on the trail, and then the anticipated, expected happened. I didn't have to tell the rebel child to look; he was beginning to be captured by the sight and sound of something special. He just didn't know what yet.

The horses rounded the distant corner, their breath signaling the labor they were giving to pull a sleigh of caroling laughing people, who were now, for a moment, a temporary family. The moon was lighting the way. The campfire, as if on cue, cracked, and again on a secret signal the coyote howled, as if giving approval to the sight of something from the past.

"Watch, listen, remember, this is something you may never see again in your life," I warned this softening rebel child. He stood, looked, and continued to watch the scene unfold before him. The effect of the magic of the mountains seeped into his memory.

As the sleigh stopped, the passengers hopped off. We retrieved the canisters of hot chocolate and the ingredients for s'mores. The laughter continued around the roaring campfire that the rebel child helped build and was very proud of as he attended placing wood to keep the fire glowing. He joined his family, telling them the exact secret place to roast marshmallows to perfection. How he knew that I don't know, but he claimed the knowledge. He was now part of his family at a different level.

Soon the fire started dying down, signaling a departure of the sleigh back to the lodge. "I want to ride the sleigh with my family," he said as he claimed space on the hay wagon. That was my hopeful goal that he would join the family for the sleigh ride back. With a snap of the reins and a command from the driver, the sleigh was on the return trip. There was one more passenger and one more family together than at the beginning of the ride.

I doused the fire with snow, listening to the final protesting noises of what was once and now is not. The silence of the mountains again claimed victory over the din of humanity. I was alone in a winter hush, broken only by the sound of my breath and feet compacting the snow. The event was over. Memories were created to be remembered on some day at a specific time when the mind wants to recall a time of life change. Not a substantial difference but a small one. People were being people together, families together.

I started the snowmobile. The insulting noise of the engine fired to life. Every moment built up to serve a purpose, and the rebel child was now a family's son. The heat of the campfire, the singing, and the chill of the evening was replaced by the recollection of family, and the memories created this winter's event.

It was an evening of comfort and direction. Perhaps it is said by Piglet talking to Winnie the Pooh, "If you weren't you, then we'd all be a bit less we." I believe the rebel child learned that lesson on a cold winter's night high in the Colorado Rockies.

Pinewood Christmas Tree

When the angels had left them and gone into heaven, the shepherds said to one another, "Let's go to Bethlehem and see this thing that has happened, which the Lord has told us about."
—Luke 2:15

The snow fell like soft white feathers from heaven. The air was crisp, and there was little, if any, breeze, Christmastime at Snow Mountain Ranch.

Every year, families would choose to celebrate Christmas at Snow Mountain. The winter staff would respond with a Christmas Eve service and the decorating of a tall just-cut Christmas tree. But I am ahead of myself.

The days before Christmas Eve, the craft shop was busy with decorations for the tree that was in Pinewood Lodge's lobby. It was undecorated. Lights had been placed on the tree, but no ornaments, for those were being crafted by the staff, families, and others during the week before Christmas.

A tradition had been started to bring new decorations to adorn the Christmas tree, and they would be new each year. None of the decorations would be used the next year. Guests were encouraged to take them home, give them away, or exchange them with other families or staff. It was a time of giving.

Glenn Tilghman was "volunteered" to find the perfect tree of massive height and symmetry that would be placed in front of the vaulted windows in the lobby. Because of the height, many of the branches on what would be the backside were trimmed and used for garland in other parts of the lodge.

The event of getting the Christmas tree in the lobby was in itself a program item. Because of the tree's girth and the width of the entrance doors, there was a lot of pulling, twisting, and some shoving. This always posed the question, how do you shove the top of a

Christmas tree? Guests and staff would help get the Tannenbaum treat in the building. A stand would have to be crafted in the lobby, and more often than not, the tree was not exactly straight up and would be anchored to one of the posts between the windows.

The aroma of a just-cut ready-to-decorate tree welcomed the senses of all who came into the building. This signaled the start of something bigger and better than the traditional Christmas a person would have at home. You were in a different place, different than being home as all the usual trappings, activities, commitments were miles away. There were new experiences, various memories, and snow activities to choose from. The fresh-cut tree somehow told you that. The massive over-fifteen-foot tree stood as a pine sentinel, proclaiming, "Christmas was just around the corner, get ready."

Once the tree was up, secured, and safe, a sign was placed stating the decoration celebration for the year's Christmas tree would be held after the Christmas Eve service. Have your decorations made and ready to put on the tree.

Not to be outdone, or excluded, the kitchen crew would prepare a buffet of refreshments, cookies, coffee, punch, and fruit. After all, this was Christmas, a time to celebrate Jesus's birth. Somehow chocolate chip, snickerdoodles, and oatmeal cookies became the nutritional fare for the evening, along with unlimited hot chocolate.

When the evening worship service was finished, the families would gather in the lobby, each with refreshments in one hand, and their one or two decorations in their other hand. Each ornament was placed on the tallest tree most people had ever seen. A family member would share where they were from, a statement about the decoration they made, and then select a place on the tree to put their ornament. Often, the children would choose the placement, and the parent, because it was high up, would gather the small child up, climb the ladder, and place the decoration in the perfect spot.

A handmade paper star was set on the uppermost part of the tree. Some families made popcorn strings or paper chains, others wooden ornaments. Others took Christmas cards and strung them together.

With each family placement, the tree became more and more representative of Christmas.

You could hear in your soul the essence of Christmas. Memorized hymns of the season would be started by a few and sung by many. The organization of music was not from a person or an individual, but from the mountain family that would be family for the event. This experience was an occasion once, and only once, in a lifetime. It was a short moment in time, yet frozen in the memory and hearts of all that were present.

Many parents would bring a gift for their kids or other children to open after the decoration of the lobby Christmas tree was finished.

For the winter seasonal staff, the lobby tree, the decorations, the gathering of families helped them create a new Christmas memory. Many were away from home for Christmas for the first time. Several families sensed the winter staff would be away from friends and relatives, and the response was for a family to invite some winter staff to their cabin for a continued Christmas celebration.

After the decorations were placed and the explanation and sharing of the ornament were completed, the lights in the lobby were dimmed. The noise of the love of an instant family was silenced for only a brief moment as the lights of the tree for the first time were turned on. A collective gasp was heard. Someone would start to sing "Silent Night," and the building was filled with the notes of Christmas.

As there is always a beginning, there must be an ending, and this evening was no exception. The presents were gathered up, wrapping paper addressed, one last cookie and hot chocolate consumed, and staff and guests were off to their temporary Christmas home. Evening over.

Standing in now an empty lobby, I would look up at the tree with human love displayed in ornaments and lights. The Christmas tree lights would be left on for a little longer. The quiet, peaceful feeling was overwhelming and comforting. It was the Christmas season where families created new memories and remembered events from the past.

Yet isn't this a lot like many first Christmas celebrations? I thought. The anticipation of the tree, the placement of the tree. Then came the families, like the shepherds, the wise men, placing gifts on, under, and around the Christmas tree. The tree representing Christ and the families the gift givers. The singing of hymns like the angels proclaiming Jesus's birth? Even the refreshments, a form of communion together on a mountaintop, covered with the silent falling of snow, protecting, nourishing the ground.

Finally, I turned the tree lights off and listened to the silence. I put on my winter coat and woke up my young daughter, who was full of cocoa, cookies, candy, and who knows what else. We walked to the door slowly, not wanting the evening's magic feelings to end but knowing they would. Yet the memory would always be there and would be repeated again next year with a new tree, more new mountain families, and another winter staff. What would be consistent was the meaning of Christmas. With that thought, we walked to the car and drove home to have our personal family Christmas.

"Daddy, will Christmas always be like this?" my daughter asked. I could not say for sure, but I did tell her there will always be a Christmas. For now, that is all that counts.

The Day after Christmas

Group Check-In at Snow Mountain Ranch

Offer hospitality to one another without grumbling.
—1 Peter 4:9

Again, like before, snow from the heavenly skies. The atmosphere is a cold grey as the sun starts to disappear. "I have not seen the sun most of the day, so how could it disappear?" I think. This is going to be a good storm, lasting all through the night and perhaps through tomorrow.

"This is what it is all about," I think as I watch the snow pile up outside my office window in Pinewood Lodge. It is December 26, and the college and high school groups will be arriving throughout the night. We are going to be at just over full occupancy, which means looking for a few extra beds. That is the game we play, book until we are full and wait for the ski groups' leaders to tell us just how many are in their group.

The staff is ready, like an army awaiting the invasion of its territory; we are all prepared to serve. There are college students from all walks of life and educational disciplines and full-time staff, some who just came for a summer and now are here for a career. They are joined by volunteers and some former staff members who come to Snow Mountain Ranch for Christmas just so they can ski.

Ellen Hay, housekeeping manager, has completed her work, and all the lodge rooms are ready. Ron Snyder, food service manager, is busy in the kitchen knowing some groups will arrive late and will want to eat. It is not his favorite scenario, but it is part of the Snow Mountain Ranch ski package. Well-fed youth sleep better, and we are a service organization. All the staff wants the best experience for each conference. Dick Engle, the camp director, is ready to help plow snow with Glen Tilghman, maintenance manager.

The lodge roof is warm from the building's heat, and the melted snow starts manufacturing icicles that will grow through the night into four- or five-foot stalactites. Their downward growth halts only when people snap them off. I sometimes wonder what would happen if they were allowed to grow and join the frozen ground. Would they last until spring?

Dark are the skies, quiet. The snow is quiet and loud. The pounding of the road grader can be heard as Glen continues the vigil of moving masses of white champagne, as the ski industry calls falling snow. I can see the headlights of the grader in the swirl of snow.

Maury calls from the ski rental center. He doesn't really have to call. He can yell the two hundred yards from the ski shop and be heard and understood. I know because I made a bet once that Maury could, in fact, do that. I won. That's why former KOA radio announcer and personality Pete Smythe named him Foghorn Flanagan.

The snow continues to fall even harder, which it often does in the evening. Pine tree branches bend under the weight, and the few streetlights are losing the battle to illuminate the parking lot, which Glen has plowed for the umpteenth time.

Headlights start to appear through the swirling snow. Like a migration of machines, one bus and then another arrives. The buses find a parking place on the recently plowed lot. The buses are filled with future skiers. From inside their warm cocoon of travel, the excited, now-uncontained passengers erupt with youthful, unbounded energy. There are high school and college groups primarily from Texas, Kansas, and Nebraska. They've come to ski the white powder snow of Winter Park Ski area.

There is something about the excitement that flatlanders feel coming to the mountains of Colorado. As if the undiscovered treasure of being in snow country becomes an annual event for many. They are here now, ready for a downhill adventure. It is evening, and they must wait until morning light. It is up to the group leaders to contain the energy and direct it toward something memorable.

The afternoon of watching the gentle snowfall has now turned into chaos. For several hours the arrival and check in continue.

Group after group continues to arrive, ready for a winter's worth of excitement. Finally, close to midnight, the last of the conference groups are secure in their rooms, skis in hand, and tired travelers are out of snowballs to hurl at each other.

It is late. I'm exhausted. I have the satisfaction of knowing that the Snow Mountain Ranch staff has done a stellar job once again. We are Team SMR. We have found a bed for the unexpected arrivals, fitted all for skis, and somehow filled those empty stomachs. Over the next few days, Snow Mountain Ranch will foster an atmosphere to create lifetime memories for youth to take back to their schools and churches. A snowball hits my window with a thud that should have broken the glass. The window is and will always be a target, as a teenage girl squeals in delight. She aimed and hit her mark as the group leader, sitting safely in my office, senses he needs to get out there and calm things down. With forty-five kids to one group leader, and considering the snowball ratio, he will pay the price first.

Christmas vacation has officially started.

SNOW SLIDE AT THE ROLLER RINK

A Time When Snow Can Be Challenging

In peace I will lie down and sleep, for you alone, LORD, make me dwell in safety.

—Psalm 4:8

The Bays in 1975, as they are still called. The staff has domiciled here now for close to 50 years. Shown in this photo is summer staff member, Kay (Gaston) Jipp, and Julie (Larson) Schwartz both from Iowa. (Photo courtesy of Kay Jipp)

Sometimes you just get lucky. That is not entirely accurate. You have been blessed by the grace of God. His timing is always perfect.

The roller rink, named the Kiva Center, housed summer staff under the roller rink for several years and, in other years, ski groups. The accommodations were not the most glorious, but they were functional. When you came to ski, by the end of the day, all a person was looking for was a comfortable, horizontal place to sleep and recoup from the downslope day.

Groups liked the modest economic of accommodations, bathrooms, showers, a bed, and generally a sound night's sleep. Today they are still called the bays and now are used for staff. However, for many groups, this housing was the best way to afford a youth ski trip. The rooms booked quickly. There was an entrance to your bay on the lower south side of the building. This meant the parking spaces would melt faster than other areas. It also allowed the metal roof of the building to do the same thing. Most times this was a watery grave for snow. Every once in a while there would be sliding of snow from the roof. Gravity is a beautiful thing unless you are the recipient of the falling snow from two stories high.

The night before, the valley had experienced a phenomenal heavy wet spring snowfall. New spring powder was adorning the ski area as well as the roofs of cabins and lodges. Maintenance had said there was going to be some snow slides off the metal roofs and to expect a few calls concerning the issue. The sun was shining most of the day, and by afternoon it was a beautiful, warm, sunny spring day. Sporadically you would hear the quiet thunder of falling snow from pine branches and occasionally from lodge and cabin roofs.

Dinner was close to being served, and the starving skiing hordes were lining up for the evening offering. When the weather was warmer, groups didn't mind standing outside waiting for the nourishment of that evening meal. Stomachs were growling, and it was a social and bragging time about the number of runs one had made, where they found the best snow, the usual ski talk.

I decided to take a drive around the property to see if there was anything that needed attention or an issue that was to be addressed.

Driving up to the cabin area, I could see where a lot of snow was pushed back from maintenance, keeping not only the roads open but where cars would park as well. I also noticed many of the southern portions of the roof of the cabins were void of the snow as would be expected.

The roller rink was next and then back to the office for supporting the evening needs of guests and group concerns. Driving along the south side of the roller rink, I saw that the parking lot was muddy. The snow had been subject to a warm day, and last night's storm left several inches of snow on the roof. The cement walks to the bay doors were dry. The awning overhang that had been constructed was doing the job it was designed to do, keeping the snow away from the bay doors. Then it happened. I heard the sliding of snow and saw the destruction of the protective awning as the snow's speed, weight, and volume tore it off the building. As the cover came down, it blocked every door of the seven bays, efficiently trapping anyone inside. What also worried me was the possibility of a guest trapped under the debris of wood, metal, and poles, to say nothing about the snow. A sick feeling in my stomach came over me and, breaking out in a sweat, sent a chill down my spine seeing what I had just witnessed. I sat stunned for a moment, looking at the catastrophe and the rubble.

I grabbed my microphone from the two-way radio. "Office, this is Bob, I need maintenance, Dick, and anyone else to the bays at the Roller Rink. The porch awning has collapsed from a snow slide." All I heard was silence from the radio; I called again and then for the third time, each time my voice sounding more and more desperate.

Finally, there was an answer, of which my reply was, "One of you better come and see for yourself as this is real." It was severe, and the situation needed to be dealt with and solved. A few moments, Dick arrived on the scene in his car and looked. He then realized the magnitude of the situation and called for maintenance and staff to help.

There was little or no way to access if anyone was trapped under the rubble. We were all praying this was not the case, yet we needed to assume the delicateness of removing any debris could cause further harm to someone.

As divine intervention would have it, the porch awning seemed to have collapsed in a few pieces and was intact, possibly leaving room for an unfortunate person if they were exiting the bay door at the time of the incident.

Being springtime, there was late afternoon light, which made the task of looking and removing the now worthless awning easier. Maintenance had arrived with the small dozer, and Glen, with the delicateness of a surgeon, started to peel back the structure almost an inch at a time.

One of the staff had managed to crawl under each section to search for anyone who might have been caught in the collapse of the awning. It was almost inch by inch, then foot by foot that the pieces of the structure were removed. What was before the parking lot was now a final resting place for the destroyed awning.

Each moment, every movement revealed the answer to prayers as no one had been injured. It seemed these hungry skiers had lined up and were being fed the evening meal. With the spring weather, people were not concerned about waiting in line.

Again, as in many times, God protected not only SMR but the various groups staying in the bays. By the time the well-fed, tired, and worn-out skiers came back to the bays, maintenance had removed most of the debris. The entrance doors were operational, although a few had some new markings from the impact of the awning's descent.

The awning was constructed well. It had held for several snow seasons, but the spring snow heavy with moisture, a sliding metal roof designed to a release mini-avalanche, and a warm spring day were the perfect trifecta for such an incident. If the snow has slid earlier, there was the potential for bodily harm. If the slide had happened during the night, it would have had the potential of trapping many individuals, although the back hallway would have provided an alternate exit.

We were not lucky that day—we were blessed. Blessed with timing, blessed with a staff that rallied to solve a critical situation quickly. Blessed with hungry skiers, and blessed to be a part of something far more significant and much higher than us.

God's grace and mercy prevailed and created a great tale for the groups to relate to those who now wished they had been on the ski trip.

Just Ranch Stories

Birthday with Rudy

*Watch and pray so that you will not fall into temptation.
The spirit is willing, but the flesh is weak.*
—Matthew 26:41

Birthdays arrive each year at the same time; we all know this. We also realize that with each birthday, memories are made. When we were younger, there was the surprise of presents such as toys, dolls, or bicycles, and as we reached our teenage years, cards with a check or cash in them.

When we became an adult, well past the age of twenty-one, many times it was dinner out and maybe a movie. Birthdays change, but memories are always there from the toy you wanted to the meal you loved and the desert you didn't need but were tempted and ordered, even though you knew you should not.

Having a birthday on April 1 brings a new set of opportunities for family and friends and raises the level of participation for jokes, pranks, innuendos, and general fun at the expense of oneself. That is always the case, and always will be. Working at SMR and being at the job on your birthday always was a day of ever-increasing merriment. One year I was presented with an emergency medical technician cake. Another year a bikini cake. Phone calls many times would start in the early hours of four o'clock and finish at midnight.

Each year I would look to find ways to keep damage control at a lower level. Each year that never happened. Would I change anything? Not in the least. Each birthday celebration was in good fun, and life is supposed to be fun. So for all the pointy hats, sparkling candles, and non-extinguishable candles, the "chocolate" cake that was not precisely chocolate, I count it all joy; after all, it was *my* birthday.

One birthday, around 1978, however, does come to mind. I had managed to not be present working this particular day and was thankful for a quiet celebration with a few friends. The day was uneventful, comfortable, and quiet, or so I thought. I remembered I needed some eggs and had planned on going to the Just Ranch to see Clarabelle and candle a dozen eggs. It was a simple errand, easy trip about a mile or so down the road, nothing to it.

I got in my car and drove to the ranch. Rudy was finishing up the afternoon chores, and I could see Clarabelle working in the kitchen. I told Rudy I would gather some eggs from the coup, bring them inside to the kitchen, candle them, pay fifty cents, and be on my way. That was the plan I had.

Gathering eggs is a fun experience. You are on a guaranteed treasure hunt. You rummage around where the chickens come to roost and lay their eggs. Generally, a search in the nest will be rewarded with your bounty of eggs, of which you have gathered in the prescribed pail. Back at the homestead log cabin turned into a house, you candle the eggs. This consists of placing the egg on a device that has a low wattage light in it and looking to be sure the egg is not a potential baby chick. You turn the egg around several times and confirm you have an egg and not an embryo. Then in the egg carton, the orb goes until you have the dozen or more you wanted.

As you check each egg, there is time for conversation. Clarabelle and I shared about the goings-on in town, the county, friends, and family. That is where I let the meaning of April 1 slip, stating it was my birthday.

Clarabelle was pulling two loaves of bread from the wood-burning oven. The whole house had the aroma of a bakery. The crackling of the stove fire and the loving warmth of the building wrapped around you felt like a favorite blanket. "Well, I didn't realize this was your birthday," Clarabelle stated. "Here, take this loaf of bread for your birthday."

Having freshly baked bread from a mountain expert cooked to perfection in a wood-burning, cast-iron stove is indeed a worthy and an excellent birthday present. I accepted, anticipating a feast of toast with jam and jelly. It was a good day to live in the mountains.

Rudy had finished his chores and was coming inside to get warm. I was ready to take my eggs and bread and go home. "Rudy, this is Bob's birthday!" exclaimed Clarabelle, like I was one of her children. Rudy looked at me, smiled, and with that ever-present sparkle in his eyes, stated, "Well, hell, this is cause for celebration." He marched over to a nondescript cabinet, opened the door, and there on the shelf was what I assumed was an unopened bottle of Jack Daniel's whiskey. In moves that would make Olympians jealous, he grabbed three glasses, set the bottle on the table, saw the bread, and asked Clarabelle to join us as soon as she brought out the homemade apple butter that we could have with my gifted loaf of bread. He did all of this while opening the whiskey bottle and proceeded to pour a mountain man double portion of this elixir.

You could tell from the aroma this "whiskey" was not the ordinary proof; the odor alone tells you that. Clarabelle brought the apple butter. "I made this the other day, have as much as you want," she stated as my birthday loaf was being sacrificed into slices for all of us. There was the aroma of *whiskey*, homemade bread, and apple butter. My thinking was the bread and butter would be a buffer for Rudy's buddy, Mr. Daniel. This was not the clearest thinking I realized about an hour later. The bread was consumed, and Mr. Daniel was not offering any more conversation. By this time, I was using my fingers to scrape the last of the apple butter out of the jar; somehow it tasted better on the bread than my fingers, I thought as my head swirled and my mushy brain worked to compensate for the loss of logic that I had displayed.

Rudy was talking away about the "good old days." Clarabelle, well, she was enjoying the moment too. I was thinking I needed to get going and go home if I could, but figure out where that might be.

As I left on wobbly legs, holding ever so carefully my treasured eggs, I thanked them both for the exceptional impromptu birthday party and present. Between the three of us, we consumed a small jar of apple butter, some homemade butter, an excellent loaf of bread, and a good portion (well, Rudy more than myself and Clarabelle) of that whiskey bottle. Rudy was rock solid, and I was like quicksand, thankful my drive home was about five thousand feet and a straight line.

Many times, in life you are tempted. You have a choice to repel the temptation or embrace the moment. It was at that moment I decided a little bit would be okay, but my definition of *small* and Rudy's were polar opposites. Every time I looked away, my glass was replenished, at least that is what I recall through my foggy memory.

I aged more than just a year that day and the next as I nursed a headache. Going to work was a challenge. While I was walking into my workspace, the world continued to pound on in my head. I was met with laughter and well wishes. It seems Rudy, being concerned for me, called the SMR office and talked to Dick Engle, and from that moment, the cat was out of the bag. It was a birthday to remember—well, remember what I could.

Good friends, celebration, joy, and now, another year older and just a bit wiser. The next several days Rudy kept apologizing, and he never offered to celebrate my birthday that way again.

Deer Meat on the Table

Though one may be overpowered, two can defend themselves.
A cord of three strands is not quickly broken.
—Ecclesiastes 4:12

Some gifts you receive you really wonder if they are a gift at all. I am not talking about the birthday tie or the ugly seasonal sweater, not to mention what your parents would sometimes give you and you opened it in front of the family.

When you live in a rural area, almost everyone is a hunter. Gun racks in the back window of trucks is a clear indication of who hunts. Hunting season in Grand County is in the fall, and people travel from all over to find the elusive elk, deer, occasional bear, or often a steak at the local restaurant when the hunt is not as successful as planned.

One season a transplanted local citizen was inquiring where a successful place to hunt deer might be. He knew that I knew because of previous conversations and the fact I had lived in the area for several years and understood reasonable hunting grounds. We talked for a while about places he could go and secure a winter's supply of meat for himself and his pregnant wife.

I didn't think of our conversation for several days until I received a call that he had been successful in his quest to become a temporary mountain man and secured meat for the winter. He went on to tell me his wife could not stand the smell of the animal. The only option was the winter's meals would be immediately removed from hanging in the garage. Just because the hunt was a success, didn't mean the reward deer on the dinner table would be tolerated, period.

"How would you like some deer meat?" was the question, of which I agreed would be good. I said I would pick it up at their home. "I would not think of it, you are doing me a favor. I will bring it to your house," he replied.

As groups were due to arrive and I was on duty, I told him to leave what he was giving me in my fridge or freezer. I thought it odd that he agreed but in an unusual way. I let it go at that, thinking nothing of it until I got a phone call at work stating there was about a half a deer on my kitchen table, that it was ready to be butchered and what I was going to do about the deer.

I don't do field surgery, not on wild animals. I was informed, not so delicately, with the family dog raising a barking fit in the background, the deer needed to be dealt with, yesterday. That was a conundrum for a solution. Groups were arriving, I could not leave, and there was hunting evidence hanging over my dining table.

That is when I called Rudy and Clarabelle. I explained the issue and the urgency of the situation. I admitted to them, although I suspect they already knew, I had no idea what to do with this half an animal. In desperation, I pleaded with them to come and take this creature off my kitchen table. If they would like to leave me a roast, that would be good. Clarabelle laughed and said they would be right up and solve the situation.

When I arrived at home later that night, there was no evidence of hunting murder in the house. My daughter was asleep, and the family pet was not trying to get a free meal or protecting the family from half a deer. All was back to normal. However, there was a note on the table stating the freezer was full of butchered meat. It was labeled as to roasts, deer burger, chuck, and deer knuckles. Also, included were recipes and ways to prepare the bounty, including the making of deer knuckle soup. The note ended with an apology that the dining room table was a bit scarred from the butcher saw when Rudy was slicing and dicing up the unfortunate animal.

We had enough meat for the winter and through the spring.

Rudy and Clarabelle once again had been there in a crisis for me and a routine day for them. I saw the couple a few days later and thanked them for solving my emergency that was not their emergency. As usual, the response was, "Neighbors helping neighbors." That was the norm for living in Middle Park and other mountain areas. People help and support people.

A skill you have is a talent you can use because someone else is proficient in other areas that you are not knowledgeable in. Nothing is required in exchange; no debt is tallied up. It is the gift of neighboring, the comfort of knowing each person has the other's back.

There was a degree of opposite lifestyles in Grand County. The ranchers, with their set of values, and the developing mountain ski home community. The continued development of ski slopes was encroaching on a ranching lifestyle that had been the norm for decades. How difficult it must have been for the generations of people who lived there as ranchers, relying on each other and the local commerce to survive to see the constant change in their community.

I also can understand now the Justs' supportive help to smooth the emotional rough spots of concern about their homestead being purchased and soon developed into a family conference center. They, I imagine, must have talked to the other ranchers and business owners in the valley. With change comes challenges, yet over time the two lifestyles found a way to appreciate each other.

This was displayed, for example, in my neighbors coming to my aid or completing a chore/service I had no idea how to do or what to do. I firmly believe Rudy and Clarabelle also did the same in helping the Y enter the community. That expression of commitment was also carried over from the Justs in the many amenities Snow Mountain Ranch gave the community. There is tremendous strength in people, families, and groups as a team working together.

As for my friend that gave me a gift that needed a bit of butchering, I thanked him for thinking of me in such a huge way. I am sure his wife, now rid of the hunt evidence, was happier. I am sure he was. We dined well for the winter. We shared what bounty we had with others as we heard and saw the need.

In the late spring, we were gifted a large ham by my parents. More likely my mom's idea than my dad's. After all, he was a hunter in the family. I think they were feeling sorry for us and the fare of deer we had consumed for the winter's meals. The ham was a welcome change in diet.

One portion of the animal we never did get the courage, the opportunity, or the desire to try was that recipe for the deer knuckle soup. Somehow that recipe was misplaced. Or I imagine we might have ventured out and tried it.

Four Clarabelle Stories

*For the sake of my family and friends,
I will say, "Peace be within you."*

—Psalm 122:8

It is believed that Clarabelle was born and raised on the lands of the Cherokee Nation. She was a pioneer woman who knew more than she said, did as much as any ranch hand, and cared deeply about her children and family. Clarabelle was one of a kind, and it would take that same type of person to be a lifelong companion to her. That would be Rudy.

Over the years, stories about this lady rancher, tracker, cook, and ranch hand would be shared, some by Clarabelle, others by Rudy or a family member. These are four stories I remember that always got my attention when I heard them.

As much of Native American history is verbal, so are the accounts, the anecdotes of a lady who came from the plains of the American West. She traveled over the Continental Divide to work as a ranch hand and eventually partner with Rudy, one of Grand County's homesteaders.

The Bobcat and Clarabelle

Clarabelle had brothers. I believe they were older than her and would try to help her with life lessons of growing up where making a living and eating often came at the end of a rifle barrel. You needed that skill to survive. Carrabelle tells this story. "There was one day I was asked to go along with my brothers to track and hunt a bobcat that was bothering our livestock." She tells of how the brothers taught her how to follow and track the animal, using signs they say and also the family dogs to eventually tree the bobcat.

"We tracked this animal for several hours and finally got him up a tree, but the boys were not finished with the hunting lesson." It seemed they would knock the animal down with a large stick and chase it to tree after tree. After a while, according to Clarabelle, "That bobcat was kind of loopy, and when knocked out of the tree, he came a-runnin' with the dogs barking and chasing him and thought I was the tree!" She recalled, "About that time, that bobcat climbed me, cat claws out and stood atop of my head, hissing, and spitting. The boys just laughed and laughed, and there I did not know what to do."

Clarabelle would laugh about the "learning experience." She would then mention she had the scars to show about that day. But her most precious memory was hanging around, hunting, and being with her brothers.

Coyotes, Clarabelle, and a Rifle

The Just Ranch encompassed over 2,800 acres, which was home to sheep, cows, horses, and several chickens. Coyotes, on the other hand, would be more than happy to have a calf, a chicken, or a sheep for their meal. You seldom saw Rudy or Clarabelle without a rifle in their possession. That was part of being a rancher.

One time I was talking to Rudy in front of their house. It was wintertime; the cattle were domiciled in the fenced portion of the barn area. The sheep were also in their pens. This was winter practice because of cold and predator danger. Rudy, as usual, was carrying a rifle, which was for livestock protection and even the possibility of coyotes thinking he might be a meal. Winter was harsh, and the empty stomachs of a pack of coyotes were always a concern.

As we talked about a coming storm, the winter weather, we would speak in "ranch-speak," which is the language of ranchers, the dialect ranchers understand. Rudy kept looking across the valley and back again. Something was bothering him. He saw movement close to the tree line. "Look there," he said as he pointed to a group of trees several hundred yards away. "Do you see that?" "See what," I thought, "the trees?" "Look closer, there that movement, coyotes."

We watched for a little while as this pack of sharp-teethed, hungry predators stayed just out of sight, making their way across the span on their way to dinner. We knew they were there, and they knew we were watching them. We would eventually go inside. They would remain outside. Dinner could be served when we were not looking, probably lamb or chicken.

"Clarabelle, can you come here," Rudy yelled. A minute later Clarabelle was walking to where we were standing, with rifle and scope in hand. She looked across the field, saw what Rudy saw, lifted her weapon, removed the safety, took aim, adjusted the range on the scope for distance, and fired.

One coyote fell dead, the others scattered like flakes of snow in the wind into the safety of the trees and redirecting their efforts for a less lethal meal.

"What do you want?" Clarabelle asked. "Nothing now," Rudy replied. "Okay then, come on in, supper's almost ready. You too, Bob, there is plenty."

I looked at Rudy smiling proudly, then stating now he needed to go across the meadow and retrieve the coyote for the hide, a chore he had not planned on. But far better than losing one of their animals to the wild pack. Rudy looked at me, looked across the meadow where the coyote lay, and said, "That is why I don't argue with her." He headed toward the house. I had dinner plans later, but for now, dinner was going to be served at the Just Ranch, and I was not going to decline.

Mountain Man Caught in a Trap

Many of the tales Clarabelle would share were light and funny, but living and surviving in the rugged conditions of the Rocky Mountains posed threats from weather and animals. Common sense always needed to prevail.

Middle Park was blessed with an abundance of animals, and fur trappers would come in hopes of trapping many animals for their hides. Winter was the prime time for trapping because of the quality of a winter hide compared to the summer months when the animals had a lighter coat of fur. Yet in the winter, danger was also higher because of blizzards, freezing weather, and the overall challenges of traipsing through up to eight feet deep of snow.

The spring-loaded traps that were used were dangerous to the trapper and devastatingly cruel to the animal as a paw would get caught, thus trapping the animal. The mountain man would come back, perhaps a day or a week later, and check his trapline. When he found an animal caught, he would dispatch the animal, release it from the death hold, and proceed to skin and eventually tan the hide for sale.

Trapping was dangerous work. You traveled alone. Others may discover your trapline and steal your animal. The animal being secured was not pleased and could lunge toward you. Not often, but occasionally the post that the trap was secured to would break lose, and a battle for survival was on between a two-legged trapper and an angry animal with three good legs.

Clarabelle recalled one time a trapper they knew came through the ranch. He shared with them an area he was going to trap for a month or two and would drop back by on his way to the fur market when he had what he needed in furs. Months passed, and the person never came by. When spring thaw was well underway, Clarabelle and Rudy ventured out to the area where the trapper said he would be. Eventually, they found him, trapped by his own trap, both arms encased in the steel jaws of the trap he was setting. Traps are triggered like a mousetrap but with a paddle. An unsuspecting animal would step on the snare, which releases two opposing spring-loaded jaws, locking the animal in a death grip.

This person had pushed down with both hands to set the trap, which was not recommended, and the trap had snapped shut on his wrists. There was no way out.

"We saw what was, we knew what had happened. We knew the trapper but didn't know who his family was. So Rudy and I found a spot that looked like he would like and buried him there." She paused and went on, "We knew him merely as Jim, and that is what we placed on a simple marker with the date we found him."

She went on to say none of his possessions were ever found, implying another trapper might have taken them. Such was the way of the land, for some.

"So I Married Her"

Rudy was a man of few words until you got him started, then the stories would be told. One story was about how he and Clarabelle met and eventually married. Once the question was asked, Clarabelle would look at Rudy and say, "Rudy, you tell them. Your story is better than mine."

Rudy would smile and recall years past when he needed several ranch hands to put up hay, tend livestock, and help with general ranch chores for the summer and fall months.

Among the people hired was this short, stocky woman, Clarabelle. He stated that he always hired men because they would work harder and longer, but he also needed someone who could cook up a meal. Clarabelle said she could do that and more.

"I hired her, found a place for her bunk, and we went to work," stated Rudy. Over the next few months, he could see Clarabelle would outwork most of the other ranch hands and still have time to fix a meal. As time went on, one ranch hand and another would move on. Some because of the rigorous work, others just to move on, but Clarabelle stayed and continued to do what was needed.

Over time, Rudy grew to rely on this mountain woman of many talents and came to trust her as a family member, but he continued to pay her. It seemed to Rudy, as he told the story, "She was worth every penny and dime we were paying her." He went on to state that perhaps she was hanging around because she liked him, to which Clarabelle would grin as she looked at Rudy.

Money was always a challenge for a homestead. That is why a lot of homesteaders had large families, but not Rudy; it was mainly him and his mother. "I decided what I was paying her was okay, but I really could not afford to pay her, so I married her."

Clarabelle would laugh. Rudy would smile and place his arm around her. This was the only time I ever saw any physical display of affection. He would nod his head as if to say, "Yes, that is what I did, and that decision was the best decision I ever made."

They were a team, a family force surviving in the Colorado Rockies. Rudy and Clarabelle became a precise definition of family. Many other families saw that commitment in Rudy and Clarabelle's lives. I will continue to believe that perhaps this mountain ranch family helped redefine family for many others.

Rudy and Clarabelle Programs

Because we loved you so much, we were delighted to share with you not only the gospel of God but our lives as well.
—1 Thessalonians 2:8

A mainstay program at SMR was the programs Rudy and Clarabelle presented to staff, guests, and conferences. Notice the enduring look of love Rudy (R), has for Clarabelle, he never tired of hearing her tell the tales of homesteading, ranching, and hunting. They were like the sun and shadow when it came to teamwork.

Very few have lived off the land where the acreage provided shelter, food, safety, and a livelihood. When we needed supplies, we would travel on a well-developed, paved road to the supermarket or some other store.

Homesteaders had to plan trips over challenging terrain, leaving their land many times for several days to stock up on supplies. Sometimes the journey was made only once or twice a year because of the distance, considering the responsibilities on the ranch. Livestock needed to be fed and protected from animal predators looking for an easy meal.

Rudy was raised on a homestead. He didn't know any other life but ranching. He was a rancher's rancher and worked alongside his siblings and parents homesteading the land. He didn't marry Clarabelle until late in life.

Because of the knowledge of the land, the love of ranching, and the opportunity for others to learn about life cloistered in the Colorado Rockies, both in the winter and the summer, Rudy and Clarabelle were asked to share what their experience was like from a time that was being quickly forgotten.

Clarabelle was a teacher, Rudy a listener, interjecting a comment or thought occasionally. The teacher was the storyteller and held the audience in the palm of her hand for over an hour, not counting questions that would always come up.

One question generally was about schooling. "When did you go to school?" a child would ask. The answer was usually, "In the summer." But only through eighth grade, as late summer hay had to be harvested. With snow sometimes six feet or deeper, getting to school several miles away was impossible, not to mention the below-zero temperatures and the brutal wind.

"We would store up as many provisions of dry goods as we thought we would need for the winter because you never knew when you could go and resupply what you needed," Clarabelle would tell the attentive crowd. "Sometimes we would be running low on flour, and we would have to make do with what we had."

Walter G. Ruesch and the Just Family – Pictured, left to right, Water G. Ruesch, Della Just, Clarabelle Just and Rudy Just. Della settled the Just Homestead with her husband in 1893 They had six Children, with Rudy staying and working the ranch basically his whole life. (Photo from the collection of Wendel Ley)

Rudy would add that anyone who was present around mealtime was never denied a meal and many times a place to shelter for the night, or until the winter's weather subsided and they could continue to their destination. Their horse, if they had one, was taken care of like the horses that the Justs owned. That was the way, the rule, and the necessity of the land.

Houses were seldom, if ever, locked. Barns were always available for the safety of the homestead livestock and those who might be traveling through the area.

Telephones were few and far between. The opportunity of hosting company was not only a necessity but also a way to catch up on any news. Sitting around a table when the meal was complete was time for fellowship and to share what was needed.

As the Justs shared about ranch life, you could see the attention of the audience listening more with each story. Guests who were hearing Rudy and Clarabelle tell of their experiences had traveled at a high rate of speed in air-conditioned cars, with music on the radio, only to arrive at Snow Mountain Ranch rested and ready for vacation. The Justs traveled when necessary for many years in buckboard wagons to Frasier or Granby, which were several miles away, to secure supplies and then back to the ranch. Vacation was a word that was not in their vocabulary. Chores, responsibility, and survival were spoken about.

As the Justs held up various furs for people to see, Clarabelle would have a story, a tale to tell about each one. The coyote was too close to the sheep, another coyote's foot was snared in a trap. The beaver's hide represented that there were too many beaver dams being built on the streams that flowed through the ranch. Water was vital to survival not only of livestock but of mankind as well.

A bear hide was brought out and displayed. "Look at the size of this bear's paw," Clarabelle would say. "Can you imagine the power and force behind something this big?" She would continue to tell about the taking of an animal's life and that it was not done in a frivolous manner, but with the necessity for the survival of livestock and family. "You don't shoot to kill just to kill. You do what you have to keep what you have. Sometimes you lose hens and chickens, even sheep to coyotes. That is part of living on the land. Life and death happen, all for a reason." She would pause for a moment and then add, "Many times we don't know the reason for something, but we do know God has a reason, and that is good enough." Rudy would cast a look of understanding and support.

You could tell by his look that there had been, and would be, losses again and again. This understanding was part of homesteading.

As the program came to a close, Rudy and Clarabelle would answer a myriad of questions about living off the land, schooling, and any other subject that came up. Finally, a child would timidly raise their hand and ask if they could come up and feel and pet the furs of the animals. This was the question Clarabelle was waiting for as the reality of what was shared in the program was now going to become real in the memory of the people through touch. "Of course, you can, anyone can come up and feel the wild in the hides," she would say. Rudy and Clarabelle would each have animal hides to share.

Watching Clarabelle and Rudy offer a part of their lives through word and now touch, you could see the oral history as it is passed from one generation to another. Perhaps, I thought, this was not just an evening's entertainment program to offer. But it was more, much more than that. This was the giving of life experiences spanning a rural lifestyle to those who would have never known the trials, the hardships of living off the land. Now people knew much more, including the joy and love of working long, tiring days. Not only did they learn about meeting challenges and doing the daily chores, but the more than the mundane of basic living. But loving entirely, even sharing with strangers who never would have known the roots of a country forged by pioneers. That perhaps was the essence of what Rudy and Clarabelle's presentation was about.

The animal hides were packed, the last question answered, the room now empty except for a few staff helping tote boxes to their truck. History had been shared, and history had been made tonight. Lives were touched. Not only the audience's but Rudy and Clarabelle's too. They knew they were loved and appreciated, and the feeling was mutual.

Great Spirit Poem

As homesteaders, Clarabelle and Rudy were rooted to the land. Because of their love of lore, earth, each other, and all the people they met, you would hear through them the history of those who went before. Now, Clarabelle and Rudy have gone before, but not without leaving legacies such as this prayer. Clarabelle would recite the prayer at the end of the program they offered to guests. Silence would follow as each person was wrapped in their personal thoughts from listening to the program.

Clarabelle would talk about life as a rancher, homesteader, and the myriad of jobs she did. Clarabelle would convey her love, appreciation, and understanding of the Native American culture that was ingrained in her Cherokee roots. Toward the end of the program, she would have a loving distant look on her face and talk about the beauty of the land. She would share her feelings about God and how He transcends cultures and captures the hearts of mankind across the world.

Pausing, she would caress the coyote fur she was holding, talking about His creations and her quiet faith, which was continually on display.

You could sense the revelation of discovery was approaching as she shared this poem she learned as a child. Rudy would look at her with a soul filled with love and understanding. He moved closer, took his beat-up rancher hat off, and stood comfortably silent as Clarabelle recited this poem. When she finished the poem, she paused, as if to say, "Look around, appreciate all He has done and given you." She then would thank the audience and with a loving smile bid a simple farewell.

It is told that this Indian version of 23 Psalm originated from a Native American tribe in Arizona. They translated it into a universal sign language to share it with members of neighboring tribes that spoke a different dialect. Over time, a missionary translated it into an English Indian style which is what you will read here. Clarabelle would close their program with this version of 23 Psalm. Silence followed as the Holy Spirit moved through the crowd.

Great Spirit Poem

Oh, great spirit, whose voice I hear in the winds,
and whose breath gives life to all the world,
hear me.
I come before you, one of your children.
I am small and meek.
I need your strength and wisdom.
Let me walk in beauty and make my eyes ever
behold the red and purple sunset.
Make my hands respect the things you have made,
my ears sharp to hear your voice.
Make me wise so that I may know the things
you have taught my people,
the lesson you have hidden in every leaf and rock.
I seek strength not to be superior to my brothers,
but to be able to fight my greatest enemy, myself.
Make me ever ready to come to you,
with clean hands and straight eyes,
so when life fades as a fading sunset,
my spirit may come to you without shame.

Just Ranch Today, 2017

Just House 2018 – built in stages over the past 100 years, the original homestead house still stands. Although not usable at this juncture, one can get the feeling of early ranch family life by wandering around the Just Ranch. (Photo from author's collection.)

Just Ranch stands not as it did when it was a working ranch back in the 1970s but like an icon of the pioneer family who worked the land, tended to the livestock, and built the log structures, the ranch stands.

Time has taken a devastating toll on the hand-built structures. However, Colorado timber is sturdy, durable with the ingrained strength to last the brutal summer sunshine and the onslaught of winter blizzards.

Like Della, Rudy, and Clarabelle Just, the buildings are rough-hewn, held together by various compounds of chinking between the logs. Yet worn with time etching away a bit of living history each day.

There is a poultry barn, close to the two-story homestead house. Chickens were kept close as they were an easy meal for predators such as coyotes, foxes, and marmots who took advantage of edible opportunities. Now, like the other buildings, the horse barn and cattle stable are defending themselves. Gone are the animals they were intended for. Now they house the wind and wild ground squirrels and other small animals.

The implement shed roof, with various parts of tractors, wagons, and other items to work the land, is sagging, succumbing to the weight of the ages of snow and burdens of a century of service. Soon, like many abandoned structures, the roof will surrender and collapse, signaling the final impending agonizing death of a building constructed to keep safe tools to work the land. The job is now finished with this structure; others will follow.

On the unattended grounds, rusting ranch implements sit as metal sentinels, now serving no function but to merely rust away. Sizeable six-foot hay mowing cutters are there waiting on time and the scrapyard. So far, they have survived both.

I take hold of one of the handles designed to do something to cut hay. I don't know why, but holding on somehow helps me connect with Rudy and his family—somehow, but only for a split second.

It seems the invasive weed, called Russian thistle, is taking over. This rooted predator is hard to eradicate and will eventually block those who wander in the field of final, perhaps lost dreams. For now, one can avoid the sticky and prickly spines of the green- and purple-flowered weed. Soon, in a few years, that will not be the case.

Just Large Animal Barn Today – Weather has not been kind to this structure. However, the barn still stands despite intense winds, penetrating sun, and disrepair. It is a testament to the knowledge of homesteaders who built structures to withstand weather and protect their livestock. (Photo from author's collection)

Soon, other log structures will deteriorate even more. The horse barn, a large log building, still stands, but the chinking between the logs is mostly gone, allowing wind and elements in to help in the process of aging. The cow barn that held the milk and meat supply is in the same disrepair, as is the sheep barn. They are all moving toward their final structural history.

On the horse barn is a twisted piece of metal that secured the top pole of the horse gate. Long ago, who knows when the bottom sanction gave way and the gate that kept the horses in corral slid from its working place to its final resting place, leaning against the barn, waiting, just waiting.

The Just home is boarded up, windows shuttered, and doors secured and locked. What was home with picture windows looking at the Continental Divide now is a blind and empty structure. A place that once held life and safety, where for many years kerosene lamps, the light supply for the home, were replaced in time with electricity. Now the house sits in darkness.

Looking through a small boarded opening in one of the windows, you can barely see inside except for a few feet. There isn't much to see. The house that was a home is empty, void of the life it supplied and the people it kept warm and protected. Barren, lifeless, but standing firm, for now, as a testament to the veracity of the homestead pioneers that lived on this land. These people decided, chose to cultivate the wild meadows, to plant hay for the livestock, to sell the abundance, and to live a life of freedom in a place called Middle Park.

Just Homestead 1971 – Notice all the flowers that Della and Clarabelle were able to plant and grow for the brief summer days in this high country. Throughout the year, the south facing room in the house was home to Fichus Trees (not native to Colorado and not easily grown) along with many other plants. Clarabelle was known in the county for her knowledge and plant growing ability.

You can hear the wind seeping through the buildings and through the absence of the chinked openings between the logs as if it was saying, "I was here first, and I will be here last." Occasionally there is a creaking sound as a board moves or a log shifts further on what was a foundation. However, the structures still stand, defending their right to be here, on this land that yielded to a family determined to tame the ground they came to claim as home. To make a living in a raging, harsh, yet spectacular environment that offers views of God's majesty everywhere you look.

It is time to go, to leave, once again. I have departed before and will return to leave again. Each time the warmth of memories envelops me like the smiles I remember from Rudy and Clarabelle. Yet as I go, I sense a continued, more significant, more profound sadness of what I missed when Rudy, Clarabelle, and Della lived here. I lost so much by not listening and being attentive. I wasted countless opportunities for conversations and time to sit and hear of those gone before.

Now I listen to the dialogue from the wind, the deafening silence of the far distance, and absence of human life because Just Ranch is a glimmer of cherished family memories of a ranch now belonging to the ages. Rest in peace.

Final Thoughts

For we are God's handiwork, created in Christ Jesus to do good works, which God prepared in advance for us to do.
—Ephesians 2:10

The story of Snow Mountain Ranch will continue in perpetuity, that is the plan. In talking to many staff members, a reoccurring statement is continually made that the experience they had at Snow Mountain Ranch was a life-changing and altering time. Many staff perhaps found an alternative life direction or calling. Others found friends forever, while some only were in the moment of the work experience.

This book could not have been completed if it was not for the staff and guests who are the essential ingredients to create such a project. It is always an honor to have worked with every one of you. Because of your decision to work at SMR, your commitment, involvement, and enthusiasm for life in general, you created a better place for so many people.

Since 1969, Snow Mountain has employed thousands of seasonal and full-time staff. Groups and families far outnumber the staff. Each group takes away a personal set of memories that is in part who they are. Memories of the same event will vary with the individual. What I remembered and what is in your mind may be different as we relate to the same past thought. For the most part, I strived to be as accurate as I could in fact-checking.

Many of you were contacted on your thoughts of SMR and your participation while at the camp. Thank you for taking the time to crawl, walk, and sometimes run down memory lane with me. Because of your willingness to share, the book is better because you took the time. You again gave of your time, just like you did when you worked at SMR.

Thank you, Carie Essing, former historian for the YMCA of the Rockies, for opening the Lula W. Dorsey Museum. The archive room gave me the opportunity to read two decades of board minutes. Your support and permission for photographic reproduction are priceless to this project.

Also, without your statement that Snow Mountain Ranch would be celebrating fifty years of existence in 2019, along with the positive encouragement you gave as you suggested a book be written on the pioneer years, this project would have never been thought of or had wings to fly to completion. Thank you.

Jack and Lulie Melton, thank you for volunteering to read the manuscript and suggesting much-needed historic and grammar changes. Your help and encouragement mean a lot. How many decades have we known each other?

To Chelsea Oakman, publication specialist at Christian Faith Publishing, for putting up with me and all my questions, concerns, and worries. Your calming direction took much of the stress away.

I am so thankful the Lord directed me to Christian Faith Publishing. It is a blessing to work with honesty in the publishing world.

Jennifer, my daughter, thanks for listening to all my ramblings about our time living at SMR. We had a great time living there. I am thankful SMR was your first home. It was an honor to have you read many of the chapters for me.

To my wife, Barbara, who supported many trips to each facility to do research, interviews, and writing, then listening to what was written, thank you for your commitment in marriage and in this book. You are written upon my heart.

Finally, to my Lord and Savior, who gave me life along with the gift of memory and the skill of being able to place pen to paper, a continual deepening thank-you for knowing who I was before time. I pray I will continue to be a good and faithful servant to you for all the days of my life.

One final thought, in researching the decades of YMCA of the Rockies board minutes, I discovered this statement Walter G.

Ruesch, managing director from 1950 to 1980, entered into the record. This was his concluding remarks to his managing director's report. I believe this is the essence of what the YMCA of the Rockies needs to strive to accomplish:

> *The YMCA of the Rockies has been built with the vision and the ideals of many people over the years. Change is popular in today's society, and although we agree it is sometimes needed, any change should be well thought out in advance, and at no time should we lose sight of our purpose, which is to help build a Christian society.* (From the YMCA of the Rockies board minutes, November 18–21, 1971, Manager's Report)

About the Author

When We Were Pioneers is the second book Robert has written about the YMCA of the Rockies. This edition is about the beginning years of Snow Mountain Ranch. In 1971, Robert accepted a position at SMR as a full-time staff, where he served as a manager for over a decade. He has also been a journalist for several newspapers and magazines, including secular and Christian publications. Robert lives with his wife in Evergreen, Colorado, and occasionally travels in their RV. They have journeyed over three hundred thousand miles doing mission work for Christian Resort Ministries, which places chaplains in RV resorts across the United States.

CPSIA information can be obtained
at www.ICGtesting.com
Printed in the USA
JSHW010823041219
2780JS00004B/13